FREE Test Taking Tips Video/DVD Offer

To better serve you, we created videos covering test taking tips that we want to give you for FREE. **These videos cover world-class tips that will help you succeed on your test.**

We just ask that you send us feedback about this product. Please let us know what you thought about it—whether good, bad, or indifferent.

To get your **FREE videos**, you can use the QR code below or email freevideos@studyguideteam.com with "Free Videos" in the subject line and the following information in the body of the email:

  a. The title of your product

  b. Your product rating on a scale of 1-5, with 5 being the highest

  c. Your feedback about the product

If you have any questions or concerns, please don't hesitate to contact us at info@studyguideteam.com.

Thank you!

New York City Police Officer Exam Study Guide

Prep Book with Practice Test Questions
[Includes Detailed Answer Explanations]

Lydia Morrison

Interested in buying more than 10 copies of our product? Contact us about bulk discounts:
bulkorders@studyguideteam.com

ISBN 13: 9781637757703

Table of Contents

Welcome 1
   FREE Videos/DVD OFFER--- 1

Quick Overview 2

Test-Taking Strategies 3

Introduction 7

Study Prep Plan for the NYPD Exam 8

Written Comprehension 9
   Finding Evidence in a Passage --------------------------------------- 9
   Author's Use of Evidence to Support Claims ------------------------11
   Rhetorical Questions --12
   Practice Quiz--17
   Answer Explanations ---19

Written Expression 20
   Clarity--20
   Spelling--29
   Vocabulary ---35
   Practice Quiz---42
   Answer Explanations --43

Memorization.. 44
   Interpreting Visual Depictions of Traffic Incidents ---------------------45
   Recognizing and Identifying Facial Features---------------------------45
   Visualizing and Identifying Patterns and Objects----------------------46
   Recalling Information from Wanted Posters --------------------------46
   Finding the Perpetrator from a Description --------------------------47
   Identifying Meaningful Details -------------------------------------47
   Filling in Police Forms --48

Practice Quiz --49

Answer Explanations --51

Inductive Reasoning **52**

Inductive and Deductive Reasoning ---52

How to Approach Inductive Reasoning Questions --------------------------------------53

Practice Quiz --56

Answer Explanations --58

Deductive Reasoning **59**

Practice Quiz --61

Answer Explanations --63

Information Ordering and Problem Sensitivity **64**

Ordering and Managing Facts Logically --64

Problem Sensitivity--64

Identifying the Most and Least Meaningful Details in a Police Scenario ----------65

Applying Police Policies --66

Frequency of Information Questions ---66

General Information Ordering ---67

Practice Quiz --70

Answer Explanation--72

Spatial Orientation **74**

Reading Maps to Find the Quickest Route ---74

How to Approach Spatial Orientation Questions---------------------------------------74

Example Spatial Orientation Question ---75

Practice Quiz --77

Answer Explanations --80

Visualization **81**

Identifying Patterns and Objects ---81

Recognizing and Identifying Facial Features ---81

How to approach Visualizing questions--82

Practice Quiz --- 83

Answer Explanations -- 85

Practice Test **86**

Written Comprehension --- 86

Written Expression -- 92

Memorization -- 95

Inductive Reasoning -- 102

Deductive Reasoning --- 106

Information Ordering and Problem Sensitivity-- 110

Spatial Orientation -- 122

Visualization --- 127

Answer Explanations **131**

Written Comprehension --- 131

Written Expression --- 134

Memorization -- 135

Inductive Reasoning --- 136

Deductive Reasoning -- 137

Information Ordering and Problem Sensitivity--- 139

Spatial Orientation --- 150

Visualization -- 152

Welcome

Dear Reader,

Welcome to your new Test Prep Books study guide! We are pleased that you chose us to help you prepare for your exam. There are many study options to choose from, and we appreciate you choosing us. Studying can be a daunting task, but we have designed a smart, effective study guide to help prepare you for what lies ahead.

Whether you're a parent helping your child learn and grow, a high school student working hard to get into your dream college, or a nursing student studying for a complex exam, we want to help give you the tools you need to succeed. We hope this study guide gives you the skills and the confidence to thrive, and we can't thank you enough for allowing us to be part of your journey.

In an effort to continue to improve our products, we welcome feedback from our customers. We look forward to hearing from you. Suggestions, success stories, and criticisms can all be communicated by emailing us at info@studyguideteam.com.

Sincerely,
Test Prep Books Team

FREE Videos/DVD OFFER

Doing well on your exam requires both knowing the test content and understanding how to use that knowledge to do well on the test. We offer completely FREE test taking tip videos. **These videos cover world-class tips that you can use to succeed on your test.**

To get your **FREE videos**, you can use the QR code below or email freevideos@studyguideteam.com with "Free Videos" in the subject line and the following information in the body of the email:

   a. The title of your product
   b. Your product rating on a scale of 1-5, with 5 being the highest
   c. Your feedback about the product

If you have any questions or concerns, please don't hesitate to contact us at info@studyguideteam.com.

1

Quick Overview

As you draw closer to taking your exam, effective preparation becomes more and more important. Thankfully, you have this study guide to help you get ready. Use this guide to help keep your studying on track and refer to it often.

This study guide contains several key sections that will help you be successful on your exam. The guide contains tips for what you should do the night before and the day of the test. Also included are test-taking tips. Knowing the right information is not always enough. Many well-prepared test takers struggle with exams. These tips will help equip you to accurately read, assess, and answer test questions.

A large part of the guide is devoted to showing you what content to expect on the exam and to helping you better understand that content. In this guide are practice test questions so that you can see how well you have grasped the content. Then, answer explanations are provided so that you can understand why you missed certain questions.

Don't try to cram the night before you take your exam. This is not a wise strategy for a few reasons. First, your retention of the information will be low. Your time would be better used by reviewing information you already know rather than trying to learn a lot of new information. Second, you will likely become stressed as you try to gain a large amount of knowledge in a short amount of time. Third, you will be depriving yourself of sleep. So be sure to go to bed at a reasonable time the night before. Being well-rested helps you focus and remain calm.

Be sure to eat a substantial breakfast the morning of the exam. If you are taking the exam in the afternoon, be sure to have a good lunch as well. Being hungry is distracting and can make it difficult to focus. You have hopefully spent lots of time preparing for the exam. Don't let an empty stomach get in the way of success!

When travelling to the testing center, leave earlier than needed. That way, you have a buffer in case you experience any delays. This will help you remain calm and will keep you from missing your appointment time at the testing center.

 Be sure to pace yourself during the exam. Don't try to rush through the exam. There is no need to risk performing poorly on the exam just so you can leave the testing center early. Allow yourself to use all of the allotted time if needed.

Remain positive while taking the exam even if you feel like you are performing poorly. Thinking about the content you should have mastered will not help you perform better on the exam.

Once the exam is complete, take some time to relax. Even if you feel that you need to take the exam again, you will be well served by some down time before you begin studying again. It's often easier to convince yourself to study if you know that it will come with a reward!

2

Test-Taking Strategies

1. Predicting the Answer

When you feel confident in your preparation for a multiple-choice test, try predicting the answer before reading the answer choices. This is especially useful on questions that test objective factual knowledge. By predicting the answer before reading the available choices, you eliminate the possibility that you will be distracted or led astray by an incorrect answer choice. You will feel more confident in your selection if you read the question, predict the answer, and then find your prediction among the answer choices. After using this strategy, be sure to still read all of the answer choices carefully and completely. If you feel unprepared, you should not attempt to predict the answers. This would be a waste of time and an opportunity for your mind to wander in the wrong direction.

2. Reading the Whole Question

Too often, test takers scan a multiple-choice question, recognize a few familiar words, and immediately jump to the answer choices. Test authors are aware of this common impatience, and they will sometimes prey upon it. For instance, a test author might subtly turn the question into a negative, or he or she might redirect the focus of the question right at the end. The only way to avoid falling into these traps is to read the entirety of the question carefully before reading the answer choices.

3. Looking for Wrong Answers

Long and complicated multiple-choice questions can be intimidating. One way to simplify a difficult multiple-choice question is to eliminate all of the answer choices that are clearly wrong. In most sets of answers, there will be at least one selection that can be dismissed right away. If the test is administered on paper, the test taker could draw a line through it to indicate that it may be ignored; otherwise, the test taker will have to perform this operation mentally or on scratch paper. In either case, once the obviously incorrect answers have been eliminated, the remaining choices may be considered. Sometimes identifying the clearly wrong answers will give the test taker some information about the correct answer. For instance, if one of the remaining answer choices is a direct opposite of one of the eliminated answer choices, it may well be the correct answer. The opposite of obviously wrong is obviously right! Of course, this is not always the case. Some answers are obviously incorrect simply because they are irrelevant to the question being asked. Still, identifying and eliminating some incorrect answer choices is a good way to simplify a multiple-choice question.

4. Don't Overanalyze

Anxious test takers often overanalyze questions. When you are nervous, your brain will often run wild, causing you to make associations and discover clues that don't actually exist. If you feel that this may be a problem for you, do whatever you can to slow down during the test. Try taking a deep breath or counting to ten. As you read and consider the question, restrict yourself to the particular words used by the author. Avoid thought tangents about what the author *really* meant, or what he or she was *trying* to say. The only things that matter on a multiple-choice test are the words that are actually in the question. You must avoid reading too much into a multiple-choice question, or supposing that the writer meant something other than what he or she wrote.

3

5. No Need for Panic

It is wise to learn as many strategies as possible before taking a multiple-choice test, but it is likely that you will come across a few questions for which you simply don't know the answer. In this situation, avoid panicking. Because most multiple-choice tests include dozens of questions, the relative value of a single wrong answer is small. As much as possible, you should compartmentalize each question on a multiple-choice test. In other words, you should not allow your feelings about one question to affect your success on the others. When you find a question that you either don't understand or don't know how to answer, just take a deep breath and do your best. Read the entire question slowly and carefully. Try rephrasing the question a couple of different ways. Then, read all of the answer choices carefully. After eliminating obviously wrong answers, make a selection and move on to the next question.

6. Confusing Answer Choices

When working on a difficult multiple-choice question, there may be a tendency to focus on the answer choices that are the easiest to understand. Many people, whether consciously or not, gravitate to the answer choices that require the least concentration, knowledge, and memory. This is a mistake. When you come across an answer choice that is confusing, you should give it extra attention. A question might be confusing because you do not know the subject matter to which it refers. If this is the case, don't

eliminate the answer before you have affirmatively settled on another. When you come across an answer choice of this type, set it aside as you look at the remaining choices. If you can confidently assert that one of the other choices is correct, you can leave the confusing answer aside. Otherwise, you will need to take a moment to try to better understand the confusing answer choice. Rephrasing is one way to tease out the sense of a confusing answer choice.

7. Your First Instinct

Many people struggle with multiple-choice tests because they overthink the questions. If you have studied sufficiently for the test, you should be prepared to trust your first instinct once you have carefully and completely read the question and all of the answer choices. There is a great deal of research suggesting that the mind can come to the correct conclusion very quickly once it has obtained all of the relevant information. At times, it may seem to you as if your intuition is working faster even than your reasoning mind. This may in fact be true. The knowledge you obtain while studying may be retrieved from your subconscious before you have a chance to work out the associations that support it. Verify your instinct by working out the reasons that it should be trusted.

8. Key Words

Many test takers struggle with multiple-choice questions because they have poor reading comprehension skills. Quickly reading and understanding a multiple-choice question requires a mixture of skill and experience. To help with this, try jotting down a few key words and phrases on a piece of scrap paper. Doing this concentrates the process of reading and forces the mind to weigh the relative importance of the question's parts. In selecting words and phrases to write down, the test taker thinks

about the question more deeply and carefully. This is especially true for multiple-choice questions that are preceded by a long prompt.

9. Subtle Negatives

One of the oldest tricks in the multiple-choice test writer's book is to subtly reverse the meaning of a question with a word like *not* or *except*. If you are not paying attention to each word in the question, you can easily be led astray by this trick. For instance, a common question format is, "Which of the following is...?" Obviously, if the question instead is, "Which of the following is not...?," then the answer will be quite different. Even worse, the test makers are aware of the potential for this mistake and will include one answer choice that would be correct if the question were not negated or reversed. A test taker who misses the reversal will find what he or she believes to be a correct answer and will be so confident that he or she will fail to reread the question and discover the original error. The only way to avoid this is to practice a wide variety of multiple-choice questions and to pay close attention to each and every word.

10. Reading Every Answer Choice

It may seem obvious, but you should always read every one of the answer choices! Too many test takers fall into the habit of scanning the question and assuming that they understand the question because they recognize a few key words. From there, they pick the first answer choice that answers the question they believe they have read. Test takers who read all of the answer choices might discover that one of the latter answer choices is actually *more* correct. Moreover, reading all of the answer choices can remind you of facts related to the question that can help you arrive at the correct answer. Sometimes, a misstatement or incorrect detail in one of the latter answer choices will trigger your memory of the subject and will enable you to find the right answer. Failing to read all of the answer choices is like not reading all of the items on a restaurant menu: you might miss out on the perfect choice.

11. Spot the Hedges

One of the keys to success on multiple-choice tests is paying close attention to every word. This is never truer than with words like *almost*, *most*, *some*, and *sometimes*. These words are called "hedges" because they indicate that a statement is not totally true or not true in every place and time. An absolute statement will contain no hedges, but in many subjects, the answers are not always straightforward or absolute. There are always exceptions to the rules in these subjects. For this reason,

you should favor those multiple-choice questions that contain hedging language. The presence of qualifying words indicates that the author is taking special care with his or her words, which is certainly important when composing the right answer. After all, there are many ways to be wrong, but there is only one way to be right! For this reason, it is wise to avoid answers that are absolute when taking a multiple-choice test. An absolute answer is one that says things are either all one way or all another. They often include words like *every*, *always*, *best*, and *never*. If you are taking a multiple-choice test in a subject that doesn't lend itself to absolute answers, be on your guard if you see any of these words.

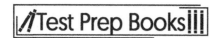

12. Long Answers

 In many subject areas, the answers are not simple. As already mentioned, the right answer often requires hedges. Another common feature of the answers to a complex or subjective question are qualifying clauses, which are groups of words that subtly modify the meaning of the sentence. If the question or answer choice describes a rule to which there are exceptions or the subject matter is complicated, ambiguous, or confusing, the correct answer will require many words in order to be expressed clearly and accurately. In essence, you should not be deterred by answer choices that seem excessively long. Oftentimes, the author of the text will not be able to write the correct answer without offering some qualifications and modifications. Your job is to read the answer choices thoroughly and completely and to select the one that most accurately and precisely answers the question.

13. Restating to Understand

Sometimes, a question on a multiple-choice test is difficult not because of what it asks but because of how it is written. If this is the case, restate the question or answer choice in different words. This process serves a couple of important purposes. First, it forces you to concentrate on the core of the question. In order to rephrase the question accurately, you have to understand it well. Rephrasing the question will concentrate your mind on the key words and ideas. Second, it will present the information to your mind in a fresh way. This process may trigger your memory and render some useful scrap of information picked up while studying.

14. True Statements

Sometimes an answer choice will be true in itself, but it does not answer the question. This is one of the main reasons why it is essential to read the question carefully and completely before proceeding to the answer choices. Too often, test takers skip ahead to the answer choices and look for true statements. Having found one of these, they are content to select it without reference to the question above. The savvy test taker will always read the entire question before turning to the answer choices. Then, having settled on a correct answer choice, he or she will refer to the original question and ensure that the selected answer is relevant. The mistake of choosing a correct-but-irrelevant answer choice is especially common on questions related to specific pieces of objective knowledge.

15. No Patterns

One of the more dangerous ideas that circulates about multiple-choice tests is that the correct answers tend to fall into patterns. These erroneous ideas range from a belief that B and C are the most common right answers, to the idea that an unprepared test-taker should answer "A-B-A-C-A-D-A-B-A." It cannot be emphasized enough that pattern-seeking of this type is exactly the WRONG way to approach a multiple-choice test. To begin with, it is highly unlikely that the test maker will plot the correct answers according to some predetermined pattern. The questions are scrambled and delivered in a random order. Furthermore, even if the test maker was following a pattern in the assignation of correct answers, there is no reason why the test taker would know which pattern he or she was using. Any attempt to discern a pattern in the answer choices is a waste of time and a distraction from the real work of taking the test. A test taker would be much better served by extra preparation before the test than by reliance on a pattern in the answers.

6

Introduction

Function of the Test

The NYC Police Department exam is for individuals who want to become New York City police officers. Every applicant must take this exam before being considered for employment. Other requirements that must be met before being hired as a police officer are:

- **Qualifying Age:** Individuals between the ages of 17 ½ and 34 can take the exam; however, the minimum age of appointment is 21 years old.

- **Education:** Applicants must have at least 60 college credit hours or have served for 2 years in an active military role.

- **Residency:** Applicants must be United States citizens; have a valid New York driver license; and live in one of the city's five boroughs or Nassau, Suffolk, Rockland, Westchester, Putnam, or Orange counties within 30 days of being hired.

Candidates who have been convicted of a felony, convicted of a domestic violence misdemeanor, or dishonorably discharged from the military will not qualify.

Test Details and Scoring

The NYPD exam consists of 55 multiple choice questions. The exam is taken on a computer. There is a 2-hour time limit for applicants to complete the exam. Once the exam is completed, the applicant will wait for their results to see whether they passed or failed. They will then be given a list number if they passed the test and continue on with the hiring process. A passing score is 70 percent or higher.

Test Sections

The NYPD exam consists of the following sections:

- Written Comprehension
- Written Expression
- Memorization
- Inductive Reasoning
- Deductive Reasoning
- Information Ordering and Problem Sensitivity
- Spatial Orientation
- Visualization

Having a strong working knowledge of these topics will give you the needed edge to walk into your exam with confidence.

Locations and Dates

There are numerous dates and times available to take the NYPD exam. Go to https://www.nyc.gov/site/nypd/careers/police-officers/po-exam.page for up-to-date information.

Study Prep Plan for the NYPD Exam

1 **Schedule -** Use one of our study schedules below or come up with one of your own.

2 **Relax -** Test anxiety can hurt even the best students. There are many ways to reduce stress. Find the one that works best for you.

3 **Execute -** Once you have a good plan in place, be sure to stick to it.

One Week Study Schedule		
Day 1	Written Comprehension
Day 2	Written Expression
Day 3	Vocabulary
Day 4	Memorization
Day 5	Information Ordering and Problem Sensitivity
Day 6	Practice Test
Day 7	Take Your Exam!

Two Week Study Schedule			
Day 1	Written Comprehension	Day 8	Deductive Reasoning
Day 2	Written Expression	Day 9	Information Ordering and Problem Sensitivity
Day 3	Spelling	Day 10	Example Spatial Orientation Question
Day 4	Vocabulary	Day 11	Identifying Patterns and Objects
Day 5	Context Clues	Day 12	Practice Test
Day 6	Memorization	Day 13	Answer Explanations
Day 7	How to Approach Inductive Reasoning Questions	Day 14	Take Your Exam!

Build your own prep plan by visiting:

testprepbooks.com/prep

8

Written Comprehension

Command of evidence, or the ability to use contextual clues, factual statements, and corroborative phrases to support an author's message or intent, is an important part of comprehending written documents. Parsing out factual information and drawing conclusions based on evidence is important to critical reading comprehension.

Finding Evidence in a Passage

The basic tenet of reading comprehension is the ability to read and understand a text. One way to understand a text is to look for information that supports the author's main idea, topic, or position statement. This information may be factual, or it may be based on the author's opinion. This section will focus on the test taker's ability to identify factual information, as opposed to opinionated bias. The PSAT/NMSQT will ask test takers to read passages containing factual information, and then logically relate those passages by drawing conclusions based on evidence.

In order to identify factual information within one or more text passages, begin by looking for statements of fact. Factual statements can be either true or false. Identifying factual statements as opposed to opinion statements is important in demonstrating full command of evidence in reading. For example, the statement *The temperature outside was unbearably hot* may seem like a fact; however, it's not. While anyone can point to a temperature gauge as factual evidence, the statement itself reflects only an opinion. Some people may find the temperature unbearably hot. Others may find it comfortably warm. Thus, the sentence, *The temperature outside was unbearably hot,* reflects the opinion of the author who found it unbearable. If the text passage followed up the sentence with atmospheric conditions indicating heat indices above 140 degrees Fahrenheit, then the reader knows there is factual information that supports the author's assertion of *unbearably hot*.

In looking for information that can be proven or disproven, it's helpful to scan for dates, numbers, timelines, equations, statistics, and other similar data within any given text passage. These types of indicators will point to proven particulars. For example, the statement, *The temperature outside was unbearably hot on that summer day, July 10, 1913,* most likely indicates factual information, even if the reader is unaware that this is the hottest day on record in the United States. Be careful when reading biased words from an author. Biased words indicate opinion, as opposed to fact. The following list contains a sampling of common biased words:

- Good/bad
- Great/greatest
- Better/best/worst
- Amazing
- Terrible/bad/awful
- Beautiful/handsome/ugly
- More/most
- Fxciting/dull/boring
- Favorite
- Very
- Probably/should/seem/possibly

Remember, most of what is written is actually opinion or carefully worded information that seems like fact when it isn't. To say, *duplicating DNA results is not cost-effective* sounds like it could be a scientific fact, but it isn't. Factual information can be verified through independent sources.

The simplest type of test question may provide a text passage, then ask the test taker to distinguish the correct factual supporting statement that best answers the corresponding question on the test. However, be aware that most questions may ask the test taker to read more than one text passage and identify which answer best supports an author's topic. While the ability to identify factual information is critical, these types of questions require the test taker to identify chunks of details, and then relate them to one another.

Displaying Analytical Thinking Skills

Analytical thinking involves being able to break down visual information into manageable portions in order to solve complex problems or process difficult concepts. This skill encompasses all aspects of command of evidence in reading comprehension.

A reader can approach analytical thinking in a series of steps. First, when approaching visual material, a reader should identify an author's thought process. Is the line of reasoning clear from the presented passage, or does it require inference and coming to a conclusion independent of the author? Next, a reader should evaluate the author's line of reasoning to determine if the logic is sound. Look for evidentiary clues and cited sources. Do these hold up under the author's argument? Third, look for bias. Bias includes generalized, emotional statements that will not hold up under scrutiny, as they are not based on fact. From there, a reader should ask if the presented evidence is trustworthy. Are the facts cited from reliable sources? Are they current? Is there any new factual information that has come to light since the passage was written that renders the argument useless? Next, a reader should carefully think about information that opposes the author's view. Do the author's arguments guide the reader to identical thoughts, or is there room for sound arguments? Finally, a reader should always be able to identify an author's conclusion and be able to weigh its effectiveness.

The ability to display analytical thinking skills while reading is key in any standardized testing situation. Test takers should be able to critically evaluate the information provided, and then answer questions related to content by using the steps above.

Making Inferences

Simply put, an inference is an educated guess drawn from evidence, logic, and reasoning. The key to making inferences is identifying clues within a passage, and then using common sense to arrive at a reasonable conclusion. Consider it "reading between the lines."

One way to make an inference is to look for main topics. When doing so, pay particular attention to any titles, headlines, or opening statements made by the author. Topic sentences or repetitive ideas can be clues in gleaning inferred ideas. For example, if a passage contains the phrase *While some consider DNA testing to be infallible, it is an inherently flawed technique,* the test taker can infer the rest of the passage will contain information that points to problems with DNA testing.

The test taker may be asked to make an inference based on prior knowledge but may also be asked to make predictions based on new ideas. For example, the test taker may have no prior knowledge of DNA other than its genetic property to replicate. However, if the reader is given passages on the flaws of DNA

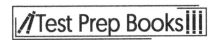

testing with enough factual evidence, the test taker may arrive at the inferred conclusion that the author does not support the infallibility of DNA testing in all identification cases.

When making inferences, it is important to remember that the critical thinking process involved must be fluid and open to change. While a reader may infer an idea from a main topic, general statement, or other clues, they must be open to receiving new information within a particular passage. New ideas presented by an author may require the test taker to alter an inference. Similarly, when asked questions that require making an inference, it's important to read the entire test passage and all of the answer options. Often, a test taker will need to refine a general inference based on new ideas that may be presented within the test itself.

Author's Use of Evidence to Support Claims

Authors utilize a wide range of techniques to tell a story or communicate information. Readers should be familiar with the most common of these techniques. Techniques of writing are also commonly known as rhetorical devices, and they are some of the evidence that authors use to support claims.

In nonfiction writing, authors employ argumentative techniques to present their opinion to readers in the most convincing way. Persuasive writing usually includes at least one type of appeal: an appeal to logic (logos), emotion (pathos), or credibility and trustworthiness (ethos). When a writer appeals to logic, they are asking readers to agree with them based on research, evidence, and an established line of reasoning. An author's argument might also appeal to readers' emotions, perhaps by including personal stories and anecdotes (a short narrative of a specific event). A final type of appeal, appeal to authority, asks the reader to agree with the author's argument on the basis of their expertise or credentials. Consider three different approaches to arguing the same opinion:

Logic (Logos)

This is an example of an appeal to logic:

> Our school should abolish its current ban on cell phone use on campus. This rule was adopted last year as an attempt to reduce class disruptions and help students focus more on their lessons. However, since the rule was enacted, there has been no change in the number of disciplinary problems in class. Therefore, the rule is ineffective and should be done away with.

The author uses evidence to disprove the logic of the school's rule (the rule was supposed to reduce discipline problems, but the number of problems has not been reduced; therefore, the rule is not working) and call for its repeal.

Emotion (Pathos)

An author's argument might also appeal to readers' emotions, perhaps by including personal stories and anecdotes. The next example presents an appeal to emotion. By sharing the personal anecdote of one student and speaking about emotional topics like family relationships, the author invokes the reader's empathy in asking them to reconsider the school rule.

> Our school should abolish its current ban on cell phone use on campus. If they aren't able to use their phones during the school day, many students feel isolated from their loved ones. For example, last semester, one student's grandmother had a heart attack in the morning. However,

because he couldn't use his cell phone, the student didn't know about his grandmother's accident until the end of the day—when she had already passed away, and it was too late to say goodbye. By preventing students from contacting their friends and family, our school is placing undue stress and anxiety on students.

Credibility (Ethos)

Finally, an appeal to authority includes a statement from a relevant expert. In this case, the author uses a doctor in the field of education to support the argument. All three examples begin from the same opinion—the school's phone ban needs to change—but rely on different argumentative styles to persuade the reader.

> Our school should abolish its current ban on cell phone use on campus. According to Dr. Bartholomew Everett, a leading educational expert, "Research studies show that cell phone usage has no real impact on student attentiveness. Rather, phones provide a valuable technological resource for learning. Schools need to learn how to integrate this new technology into their curriculum." Rather than banning phones altogether, our school should follow the advice of experts and allow students to use phones as part of their learning.

Rhetorical Questions

Another commonly used argumentative technique is asking rhetorical questions, questions that do not actually require an answer but that push the reader to consider the topic further.

> I wholly disagree with the proposal to ban restaurants from serving foods with high sugar and sodium contents. Do we really want to live in a world where the government can control what we eat? I prefer to make my own food choices.

Here, the author's rhetorical question prompts readers to put themselves in a hypothetical situation and imagine how they would feel about it.

Figurative Language

Literary texts also employ rhetorical devices. **Figurative language** like simile and metaphor is a type of rhetorical device commonly found in literature. In addition to rhetorical devices that play on the *meanings* of words, there are also rhetorical devices that use the *sounds* of words. These devices are most often found in poetry but may also be found in other types of literature and in non-fiction writing like speech texts.

Alliteration and assonance are both varieties of sound repetition. Other types of sound repetition include: **anaphora**, repetition that occurs at the beginning of the sentences; **epiphora**, repetition occurring at the end of phrases; **antimetabole**, repetition of words in reverse order; and **antiphrasis**, a form of denial of an assertion in a text.

Alliteration refers to the repetition of the first sound of each word. Recall Robert Burns' opening line:

> My love is like a red, red rose

This line includes two instances of alliteration: "love" and "like" (repeated *L* sound), as well as "red" and "rose" (repeated *R* sound). Next, assonance refers to the repetition of vowel sounds, and can occur anywhere within a word (not just the opening sound). Here is the opening of a poem by John Keats:

> When I have fears that I may cease to be

> Before my pen has glean'd my teeming brain

Assonance can be found in the words "fears," "cease," "be," "glean'd," and "teeming," all of which stress the long *E* sound. Both alliteration and assonance create a harmony that unifies the writer's language.

Another sound device is **onomatopoeia**, or words whose spelling mimics the sound they describe. Words such as "crash," "bang," and "sizzle" are all examples of onomatopoeia. Use of onomatopoetic language adds auditory imagery to the text.

Readers are probably most familiar with the technique of pun. A **pun** is a play on words, taking advantage of two words that have the same or similar pronunciation. Puns can be found throughout Shakespeare's plays, for instance:

> Now is the winter of our discontent

> Made glorious summer by this son of York

These lines from *Richard III* contain a play on words. Richard III refers to his brother, the newly crowned King Edward IV, as the "son of York," referencing their family heritage from the house of York. However, while drawing a comparison between the political climate and the weather (times of political trouble were the "winter," but now the new king brings "glorious summer"), Richard's use of the word "son" also implies another word with the same pronunciation, "sun"—so Edward IV is also like the sun, bringing light, warmth, and hope to England. Puns are a clever way for writers to suggest two meanings at once.

Counterarguments

If an author presents a differing opinion or a counterargument in order to refute it, the reader should consider how and why this information is being presented. It is meant to strengthen the original argument and shouldn't be confused with the author's intended conclusion, but it should also be considered in the reader's final evaluation.

Authors can also use bias if they ignore the opposing viewpoint or present their side in an unbalanced way. A strong argument considers the opposition and finds a way to refute it. Critical readers should look for an unfair or one-sided presentation of the argument and be skeptical, as a bias may be present. Even if this bias is unintentional, if it exists in the writing, the reader should be wary of the validity of the argument. Readers should also look for the use of stereotypes, which refer to specific groups. Stereotypes are often negative connotations about a person or place, and should always be avoided. When a critical reader finds stereotypes in a piece of writing, they should be critical of the argument, and consider the validity of anything the author presents. Stereotypes reveal a flaw in the writer's thinking and may suggest a lack of knowledge or understanding about the subject.

Meaning of Words in Context

There will be many occasions in one's reading career in which an unknown word or a word with multiple meanings will pop up. There are ways of determining what these words or phrases mean that do not require the use of the dictionary, which is especially helpful during a test where one may not be available. Even outside of the exam, knowing how to derive an understanding of a word via context clues will be a critical skill in the real world. The context is the circumstances in which a story or a passage is happening, and can usually be found in the series of words directly before or directly after the word or phrase in question. The clues are the words that hint towards the meaning of the unknown word or phrase.

There may be questions that ask about the meaning of a particular word or phrase within a passage. There are a couple ways to approach these kinds of questions:

- Define the word or phrase in a way that is easy to comprehend (using context clues).
- Try out each answer choice in place of the word.

To demonstrate, here's an example from *Alice in Wonderland*:

Alice was beginning to get very tired of sitting by her sister on the bank, and of having nothing to do: once or twice she peeped into the book her sister was reading, but it had no pictures or conversations in it, "and what is the use of a book," thought Alice, "without pictures or conversations?"

Q: As it is used in the selection, the word peeped means:

Using the first technique, before looking at the answers, define the word *peeped* using context clues and then find the matching answer. Then, analyze the entire passage in order to determine the meaning, not just the surrounding words.

To begin, imagine a blank where the word should be and put a synonym or definition there: "once or twice she _____ into the book her sister was reading." The context clue here is the book. It may be tempting to put *read* where the blank is, but notice the preposition word, *into*. One does not read *into* a book, one simply reads a book, and since reading a book requires that it is seen with a pair of eyes, then *look* would make the most sense to put into the blank: "once or twice she looked into the book her sister was reading."

Once an easy-to-understand word or synonym has been supplanted, readers should check to make sure it makes sense with the rest of the passage. What happened after she looked into the book? She thought to herself how a book without pictures or conversations is useless. This situation in its entirety makes sense.

Now check the answer choices for a match:
    a. To make a high-pitched cry
    b. To smack
    c. To look curiously
    d. To pout

Since the word was already defined, Choice *C* is the best option.

14

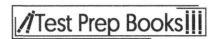

Using the second technique, replace the figurative blank with each of the answer choices and determine which one is the most appropriate. Remember to look further into the passage to clarify that they work, because they could still make sense out of context.

   a. Once or twice, she <u>made a high pitched cry</u> into the book her sister was reading
   b. Once or twice, she <u>smacked</u> into the book her sister was reading
   c. Once or twice, she <u>looked curiously</u> into the book her sister was reading
   d. Once or twice, she <u>pouted</u> into the book her sister was reading

For Choice *A*, it does not make much sense in any context for a person to cry into a book, unless maybe something terrible has happened in the story. Given that afterward Alice thinks to herself how useless a book without pictures is, this option does not make sense within context.

For Choice *B*, smacking a book someone is reading may make sense if the rest of the passage indicates a reason for doing so. If Alice was angry or her sister had shoved it in her face, then maybe smacking the book would make sense within context. However, since whatever she does with the book causes her to think, "what is the use of a book without pictures or conversations?" then answer Choice *B* is not an appropriate answer. Answer Choice *C* fits well within context, given her subsequent thoughts on the matter. Answer Choice *D* does not make sense in context or grammatically, as people do not pout into things.

This is a simple example to illustrate the techniques outlined above. There may, however, be a question in which all of the definitions are correct and also make sense out of context, in which the appropriate context clues will really need to be honed in on in order to determine the correct answer. For example, here is another passage from *Alice in Wonderland*:

> ... but when the Rabbit actually took a watch out of its waistcoat pocket, and looked at it, and then hurried on, Alice <u>started</u> to her feet, for it flashed across her mind that she had never before seen a rabbit with either a waistcoat-pocket or a watch to take out of it, and burning with curiosity, she ran across the field after it, and was just in time to see it pop down a large rabbit-hole under the hedge.

Q: As it is used in the passage, the word <u>started</u> means _____.

   a. to turn on
   b. to begin
   c. to move quickly
   d. to be surprised

All of these words qualify as a definition of *start*, but using context clues, the correct answer can be identified using one of the two techniques above. It's easy to see that one does not turn on, begin, or be surprised to one's feet. The selection also states that she "ran across the field after it," indicating that she was in a hurry. Therefore, to move quickly would make the most sense in this context.

The same strategies can be applied to vocabulary that may be completely unfamiliar. In this case, focus on the words before or after the unknown word in order to determine its definition. Take this sentence, for example:

> Sam was such a <u>miser</u> that he forced Andrew to pay him twelve cents for the candy, even though he had a large inheritance and he knew his friend was poor.

Unlike with assertion questions, for vocabulary questions, it may be necessary to apply some critical thinking skills when something isn't explicitly stated within the passage. Think about the implications of the passage, or what the text is trying to say. With this example, it is important to realize that it is considered unusually stingy for a person to demand so little money from someone instead of just letting their friend have the candy, especially if this person is already wealthy. Hence, a <u>miser</u> is a greedy or stingy individual.

Questions about complex vocabulary may not be explicitly asked, but this is a useful skill to know. If there is an unfamiliar word while reading a passage and its definition goes unknown, it is possible to miss out on a critical message that could inhibit the ability to appropriately answer the questions. Practicing this technique in daily life will sharpen this ability to derive meanings from context clues with ease.

Practice Quiz

The next two questions are based on the following passage:

A Drug Free School Zone indicates an area where drug offenses carry stricter penalties. This policy was created in the 1970s to deter citizens from committing drug crimes on or around school grounds. A Drug Free School Zone is part of federal law, but states can vary the penalties enforced on those who are convicted of drug-related violations near school campuses. What constitutes a Drug Free School Zone is determined by each jurisdiction, but typically includes school grounds, adjacent areas within 1000 feet, and school buses. Since the 1970s, all fifty states and Washington D.C. have adopted a Drug Free School Zone policy. More recently, some states have reduced the penalties, believing them to be too harsh for minor drug offenses that happened to occur near a school.

1. Based on the previous passage, which of the following statements best describes the purpose of a Drug Free School Zone?
    a. To help police locate and arrest students who are dealing drugs.
    b. To help school staff to locate and eliminate the use of drugs on campus.
    c. To deter people from committing drug-related crimes on and around schools.
    d. To eliminate the use of drugs on school buses.

2. Based on the previous passage, which of the following statements is most accurate?
    a. All fifty states have a 1000-foot zone around each school building that is designated as a Drug Free School Zone.
    b. The Drug Free School Zone enforces stricter penalties on those committed of drug-related offenses on or around school grounds.
    c. The Drug Free School Zone does not include school buses.
    d. Most states have abandoned the Drug Free School Zone policy because the penalties are too harsh.

The next two questions are based on the following passage:

Any division of government (federal, state, local) can declare a state of emergency. A state of emergency means that the government has suspended the normal constitutional procedures. In this case, citizens may not have the same rights that they typically do, such as driving on public roadways or whether they can remain in their homes. A state of emergency is typically declared in the wake of a disaster. Disasters can include hurricanes, tornadoes, floods, snowstorms, wildfires, and issues of public health such as a flu outbreak. In the event of a major snowstorm, for example, a government can issue a state of emergency to clear roads for emergency responders and to keep citizens safely in their homes. Declaring a state of emergency can also allow a government to access the use of funds, personnel, equipment, and supplies that are reserved for such a situation.

3. Based on the previous passage, which of the following statements best describes a state of emergency?
   a. The government suspends normal constitutional operations.
   b. Curfews are imposed by the government.
   c. All citizens must remain in their homes.
   d. The government can remove all citizens' rights

4. Which of the following statements is most accurate based on the preceding passage?
   a. Declaring a state of emergency guarantees states will receive federal funding.
   b. Only state government can declare a state of emergency.
   c. Declaring a state of emergency allows the government to access reserved funding, personnel, and supplies.
   d. A state of emergency does not include issues of public health.

The next question is based on the following passage:

> In the event of a riot, police officers need to be prepared with the necessary gear to manage a large and potentially dangerous crowd. Front line riot police officers are equipped with helmets, riot shields, and body armor for protection. They also may carry gas masks in the event that tear gas is used to incapacitate or disperse a crowd. Riot police officers do have firearms, but less lethal methods of crowd management are preferred. Officers have traditionally used batons and whips to manage unruly crowds. In more recent years, police have begun using more effective methods such as tear gas, pepper spray, tasers, and rubber bullets.

5. The main idea of this passage is best stated with which of the following sentences?
   a. Riot police use gas masks for protection from tear gas and pepper spray.
   b. Violent crowds should always be incapacitated with tear gas.
   c. Batons and whips are not very good methods of crowd control.
   d. Riot police must be prepared with the necessary equipment to manage a dangerous crowd.

See answers on the next page.

Answer Explanations

1. C: Based on the passage, the best description of the purpose of a Drug Free School Zone is to deter citizens from committing drug related crimes on and around school campuses. Nothing in the passage suggests the law was created to help police identify students who are dealing drugs. The laws do not help schools identify drug use on campus; they only make penalties stricter for those who do. While a Drug Free School Zone may help deter drug use on school buses, this is not the primary purpose of the policy.

2. B: Based on the passage, the most accurate statement is that Drug Free School Zones enforce stricter penalties on those committing drug offenses on or near school grounds. While some states do enforce a 1000-foot zone around schools, the passage states that this is only typically the case, and is not the case for all fifty states. The Drug Free School Zone does include buses in most states. The passage notes that some states have reduced penalties in Drug Free School Zones, deeming them too harsh, but it does not say that most states have abandoned the policy.

3. A: The statement that best defines a state of emergency is the suspension of normal constitutional operation. While a curfew may be imposed when a state of emergency is declared, this is not always the case. Citizens may need to remain in their homes, but in the case of a hurricane or flood, evacuations may be necessary, so this answer is incorrect. While a government does have a right to alter citizens' rights in a state of emergency, it is to maintain their safety, and does not extend to all of their rights as citizens.

4. C: Based on the passage, the best answer is that a state of emergency allows the government access to reserved supplies, funding, and personnel. The passage does not suggest that a state of emergency will guarantee federal funding to any government. Local, state, and federal government can declare a state of emergency. The passage states that issues of public health can be addressed with a state of emergency declaration.

5. D: This statement best captures the main idea, or main point of the paragraph, which is to show the necessary equipment police officers must have to best manage a riot. While riot police do use gas masks for protection, this is too specific to be the main idea of the paragraph. The passage mentions tear gas, but does not suggest it is the best method to manage a crowd, so this is not the main focus of the paragraph. The passage does mention that better methods of crowd control than batons and whips have been used in recent years, but this is a supporting detail, and not the main idea of the passage.

19

Written Expression

Clarity

The ability to write clearly and effectively is an important skill. Written communications such as reports are an integral part of the job, and being able to produce clear, comprehensive communications is essential. Clear written communication is important in everyday life, too.

This section of the study guide focuses on writing *clarity*. The definition of clarity is "the quality of being clear." In writing, this means that the content is focused and the writer's intention is clear in both word choice and sentence structure. Why is this important? Writers want their readers to understand exactly what they're saying and NOT misinterpret their words. In the same sense, readers want a clear understanding of what they're reading. The following section covers understanding writing clarity through basic grammar principles.

Subjects and Predicates

Subjects

Every complete sentence is made up of two parts: a subject and a predicate. The **subject** is *who* or *what* the sentence is about. There are three subject types: simple, complete, and compound.

A **simple subject** tells *who* or *what* the sentence is about without additional details. For example:

> The blue car won the race.

In this sentence, the simple subject is the word *car*.

A **complete subject** contains the simple subject and its modifiers. In writing, a **modifier** is a word or phrase that gives more detail about a part of the sentence. In this case, the modifier gives more information about the subject. When looking for a complete subject, first identify the verb or action word in the sentence (e.g., *run, jump, carried*), then ask to *who* or *what* the verb is referring. Look again at the previous example:

> Sentence: The blue car won the race.
>
> Identify the verb: *won*
>
> Ask who or what won: *The blue car*
>
> Answer: *The blue car* is the complete subject because it answers *what* won. Notice how the complete subject includes the simple subject (*car*) along with its modifier (*blue*).

If there's more than one subject in a sentence, it's called a **compound subject**. Look at the sentence below and identify the compound subject:

> Sentence: John and I jumped over the huge puddle in the parking lot.
>
> Identify the verb: *jumped*
>
> Ask who or what jumped: *John and I*

Answer: *John and I* is the compound subject of the sentence because more than one subject can answer the question of *who* jumped over the puddle.

Predicates

In a sentence, the **predicate** usually tells something about the subject by describing what the subject does, is, or has. Similar to subjects, predicates are simple, complete, or compound.

A **simple predicate** is simply the verb. For example:

The dog ran into the busy road.

In this sentence, the simple predicate is the word *ran*.

A **complete predicate** contains the verb as well as its modifiers. In the example above, the complete predicate is *ran into the busy road*.

A **compound predicate** is when two or more words describe one subject. For example:

The flight was delayed and eventually canceled.

In this sentence, the compound predicate (*was delayed and eventually canceled*) provides two details about one subject (*The flight*).

Modeling Subjects and Predicates in a Sentence Diagram

A **sentence diagram** makes it easier to identify the subject and predicate in a sentence. To create one, draw a long horizontal line with a short vertical line going through it. Write the subject of the sentence to the left of the vertical line and the predicate to the right. Here's an example:

The black pen | ran out of ink on the last page of the document.

(*SUBJECT*)　　　(*PREDICATE*)

The vertical line divides the subject (*The black pen*) from the predicate (*ran out of ink*).

Subject-Verb Agreement

The basic rule of subject-verb agreement is that a **singular subject** (one person, place, or thing) requires a singular verb, while a **plural subject** (more than one person, place, or thing) needs a plural verb.

When a sentence is in the present tense and contains a singular subject, the singular verb usually ends with the letter *s*. For example:

Riley stacks the books on the shelf.

Since the subject (*Riley*) is singular, the verb needs to be singular (*stacks*). If the subject is plural, the verb must also be plural:

Riley and Nate stack the books on the shelf.

In this sentence the subject is plural (*Riley and Nate*) so the verb must be plural (*stack*). Subjects can be nouns (as above) or pronouns. When the subject is a singular pronoun such as *I* or *you*, the verb is also

21

singular. In the case of *I* or *you*, though the verb is singular, it usually will not have an *s* on the end. For example:

Can *you call* for the pizza in ten minutes?

In this case the subject (*you*) is singular, so the verb (*call*) is also singular.

Subjects and verbs must also agree in point of view (POV) and verb tense (past, present, or future). The first-, second-, and third-person Point Of View pronouns (singular and plural) are shown below:

	First-Person POV	Second-Person POV	Third-Person POV
Singular Pronoun	*I*	*You*	*He/She/It*
Plural Pronoun	*We*	*You*	*They*

Using the chart above, look at the following examples of subject-verb agreement in relation to point of view and verb tense (in this case, present tense):

	Singular Verb	**Plural Verb**
First-Person POV	*I am swimming.*	*We are swimming.*
Second-Person POV	*You are swimming.*	*You are swimming.*
Third-Person POV	*He is swimming.*	*They are swimming.*

In each example above, the verb agrees with its singular or plural subject.

Words Between Subjects and Verbs

Interrupting words such as *of* and *to* are commonly used between subjects and verbs. For example:

The lowest point *of* his career was yesterday, when he missed the penalty shot in the playoff game.

The subject here is *lowest point*, and the verb is *was.* Notice how the phrase *of his career* doesn't influence the verb *was.*

Compound Subjects

With a compound subject there's more than one subject (plural), so the verb must be plural. For example:

Mike and Vince play basketball on Friday nights.

Notice how the compound subject (*Mike and Vince*) requires a plural verb (*play*) to agree.

Subjects Joined by *Or* or *Nor*

Singular subjects need a singular verb if they are joined by the words *or* or *nor*. If there are plural subjects, *the subject closest to the verb* determines if the verb is singular or plural. Here are examples of both:

The table or the couch arrives tomorrow.

The singular verb (*arrives*) is used because the two singular subjects (*table* and *couch*) are joined by the word *or*.

> The table or the *couches* arrive tomorrow.

In this case, the plural verb (*arrive*) is used because the subject closest to the verb (*couches*) is plural.

Indefinite Pronouns *Either, Neither,* and *Each*

In a sentence, the words *either*, *neither*, and *each* act as singular subjects. For example:

> *Neither* of the printers *is* working properly.

Since the word *neither* acts as a singular subject, the verb (*is*) must also be singular.

The Adjectives *Every* and *Any* with Compounds

If a compound word contains the adjectives *every* and *any*, it acts as a singular subject, therefore making the verb singular. For example:

> *Everyone is* here for the surprise party!

Notice how the verb (*is*) is singular because the word *everyone* begins with *every*.

Collective Nouns

Collective nouns represent a group or collection of people, places, or things. Words such as *team*, *class*, *family*, and *jury* are all examples of collective nouns. When using a collective noun in a sentence, the verb is singular if the group is working together as a whole. For example:

> Their *family is* waiting for the dog to come home.

The collective noun *family* determines the singular verb *is* instead of *are.* A simple trick would be to replace the collective noun with a pronoun. In this case, replace *Their family* with *it*, since *family* refers to a single unit.

Plural Form and Singular Meaning

Words such as *scissors*, *pants*, and *tweezers* are all examples of nouns that exist only in plural form. All are singular in meaning but plural in their structure. For plural nouns with singular meaning, the verb is singular. For example:

> The *news is* doing a special on male teachers in elementary education.

Notice how *news* seems plural but is actually singular. Therefore, it uses the singular verb *is.*

Complements

Nouns, pronouns, and adjectives can act as **complements**, providing details to complete the meaning of a sentence. These so-called "sentence completers" include predicate nominatives, predicate adjectives, direct objects, and indirect objects. It's important to note that both predicate nominatives and predicate adjectives follow *linking verbs* (e.g., *is, am, are, was, were, be, being, been*) that show no action.

Predicate Nominatives

Predicate nominatives are nouns or pronouns that rename or modify the subject and *follow a linking verb*. For example:

> My dog is a poodle.

In this sentence, the word *poodle* renames the subject (*dog*) and follows the linking verb (*is*).

Predicate Adjectives

Predicate adjectives are adjectives that rename or modify the subject and *follow a linking verb*. For example:

> My cat is lazy.

In this sentence, the word *lazy* is the predicate adjective because it modifies the subject (*cat*) and follows the linking verb (*is*).

Direct Objects

A **direct object** is a noun, pronoun, or phrase that follows an action verb and answers the question *what* or *who* about the verb. Though a sentence needs a subject and a verb to be complete, it doesn't always need a direct object. To find the direct object in a sentence, look at the following formula:

> Subject + Verb + *what*? or *who*? = Direct Object

Now, apply this formula to the following sentence:

> Spike and Sheena chased the ball around the house.
>
> Subject(s): *Spike and Sheena*
>
> Verb: *chased*
>
> Direct Object: *the ball*

Indirect Objects

An **indirect object** is a noun or pronoun that tells *to whom* or *for whom* the action of the verb is being done. A sentence must have a direct object to have an indirect object. When looking for the indirect object in a sentence, first find the verb and then ask the question *to whom* or *for whom*. For example:

> Lucy passed the crayon to her friend.

In this sentence, the indirect object is *her friend* because it answers *to whom* Lucy *passed* (verb) *the crayon* (direct object).

Pronoun Usage

A **pronoun** is a word that takes the place of a noun. This section looks at the different ways that pronouns are used in sentences.

Pronoun-Antecedent Agreement

An **antecedent** is a word or phrase that typically comes first, followed by a pronoun that refers to it. The pronoun must agree with its antecedent in form (singular or plural). For example:

> *Singular Agreement*:

> > The *package* was dropped off at my door, and *it* was very heavy.

Here the antecedent (*package*) is singular, so the pronoun (*it*) must also be singular.

> *Plural Agreement*:

> > The *packages* were dropped off at my door, and *they* were very heavy.

In this example, the antecedent (*packages*) is plural, so the pronoun (*they*) must also be in plural form.

When there are **compound subjects** (more than one subject) in a sentence, test each pronoun individually with the verb to determine which one is correct. To do this, simply remove the first subject, read the sentence with the remaining pronoun, and decide which one sounds better. For example, look at these two sentences:

> Mom and I are going to the park.

> Mom and me are going to the park.

Delete the first subject (*Mom*) from the sentences and then read them both (*I am going to the park* and *me is going to the park*). Which one sounds better? Clearly the first sentence, so the pronoun *I* is the correct choice.

25

Pronoun Reference

A pronoun shouldn't confuse the reader about whom or what it's describing, and it should clearly refer to its antecedent. For example:

Unclear: The shovel and the pail floated away in the ocean, and it was long gone.

In this sentence, it can't be determined if the pronoun *it* refers to *the shovel* or *the pail*.

Clear: The pail floated away in the ocean, and it was long gone.

In this sentence, the pronoun *it* clearly refers to its antecedent, *the pail*.

Personal Pronouns

Personal pronouns can be in the subjective, objective, or possessive case:

Subjective Case: The pronoun replaces the subject of the sentence.

Objective Case: The pronoun functions as the object.

Possessive Case: The pronoun shows possession of something.

The table below provides examples of each personal pronoun case:

Subjective	Objective	Possessive
I	Me	Mine
You	You	Yours
He	Him	His
She	Her	Hers
It	It	Its
We	Us	Ours
They	Them	Theirs
*Who	*Whom	Whose

*The pronouns *who* and *whom* are often used incorrectly. Use the pronoun *who* when referring to the *subject* of the sentence. Use the pronoun *whom* when referring to the *object* of the sentence.

In the following sentence, identify each pronoun and its case:

The flowers grew in his garden.

The pronoun is *his,* and it's in the possessive case.

Can someone please tell them to turn the music down?

The pronoun is *them,* and it's in the objective case.

Melissa is a really good cook, and she uses only fresh ingredients.

The pronoun is *she,* and it's in the subjective case.

Sentence Structures

There are many ways to organize the words in a sentence to clarify ideas. The four main sentence structures are simple sentences, compound sentences, complex sentences, and compound-complex sentences. In writing, using a variety of these structures makes the style more effective.

Simple Sentences

A **simple sentence** is made up of one independent clause. An **independent clause** is a separate complete thought that can stand on its own, and contains a subject and a predicate. Simple sentences can have compound subjects or compound verbs, but they can only have one main thought. The following is an example of a simple sentence:

> The bus was late.

The singular subject is *bus*, and the predicate is *was late*, so the sentence is a complete thought.

Compound Sentences

A **compound sentence** uses a conjunction to join two independent clauses. **Conjunctions** are linking words such as *and, but, for, nor, or, so,* and *yet*. For example:

> Bradley waited for the bus, but the bus was late.

In this sentence there are two complete thoughts (*Bradley waited for the bus* and *the bus was late*) joined by the conjunction *but*. Therefore, this is a compound sentence.

Complex Sentences

A **complex sentence** consists of one independent clause and one or more dependent clauses. A **dependent clause** is a clause that contains a subject and a verb, but can't stand on its own as a sentence. Complex sentences often use words like *after, although, before, while, wherever, if,* and *since*. For example:

> Although she really enjoyed the opera, Mary was very tired by the end of the night.

The first word in the sentence (*Although*) immediately attracts the reader's attention. The dependent clause (*Although she really enjoyed the opera*) is followed by the independent clause (*Mary was very tired by the end of the night*), which makes this a complex sentence.

Compound-Complex Sentences

A **compound-complex sentence** has at least two independent clauses and at least one dependent clause. For example:

> Although she really enjoyed the opera, Mary was very tired by the end of the night, and she still had to walk home.

The dependent clause (*Although she really enjoyed the opera*) depends on both the first independent clause (*Mary was very tired by the end of the night*) and the second independent clause (*and she still had to walk home*).

Sentence Fragments

A **sentence fragment** is an incomplete sentence that can't stand on its own. It's a dependent clause or phrase that looks like sentences but isn't. A sentence fragment may start with a capital letter and end with punctuation, but it isn't a complete thought. To revise a sentence fragment, either link the fragment to another sentence or add on to create a complete sentence. Look at the following example:

I turned off the television. Because the phone was ringing.

Fragment: *Because the phone was ringing.*

Possible revisions:

I turned off the television because the phone was ringing.

Because the phone was ringing, I ran upstairs to answer it.

Dangling and Misplaced Modifiers

Dangling Modifiers

A **dangling modifier** is a word or phrase where the word it's supposed to modify is missing. In other words, it has nothing to modify. It can also be a dependent clause that's not logically related to the word it should modify. To correct a dangling modifier, connect it to the word it's to modify. For example:

Dangling: Having designed the float for the parade, it will take six months to build it.

Revised: Having designed the float for the parade, he expects to build it in six months.

In the revision, *Having designed* now correctly modifies the subject of the sentence (*he*).

Misplaced Modifiers

A **misplaced modifier** is word or phrase that's separated from the word that it's supposed to modify. Though a modifier can be put in more than one place within a sentence, the modifier should be clearly attached to the word it describes. For example:

Misplaced: The dog almost chased the squirrel for an hour.

Revised: The dog chased the squirrel for almost an hour.

In this example, the dog didn't *almost* chase the squirrel, it *did* chase the squirrel. The revised version of the sentence connects the word *almost* to the words *an hour,* which creates the clearest meaning of the sentence.

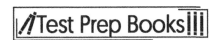

Run-On Sentences

A **run-on sentence** has two or more independent clauses that aren't connected by any punctuation. Instead, the sentence goes on and on without any pauses or stops. Here are some ways to correct a run-on sentence:

Add a comma and a coordinating conjunction:

> *Incorrect*: I loaded the dishwasher can you drain the sink?

> *Correct*: I loaded the dishwasher, so can you drain the sink?

Add a semicolon, colon, or dash (without a coordinating conjunction) when the two independent clauses are related to each other:

> *Incorrect*: I went to the movies at the snack bar I bought candy.

> *Correct*: I went to the movies; there I bought candy at the snack bar.

Separate the clauses by turning them into two separate sentences:

> *Incorrect*: The grocery store was busy it quickly sold out of bread.

> *Correct*: The grocery store was busy. It quickly sold out of bread.

Turn one of the independent clauses into a phrase:

> *Incorrect*: The grocery store was busy it quickly sold out of bread.

> *Correct*: The busy grocery store quickly sold out of bread.

Spelling

Choosing the best words for each situation is only part effective writing. Being able to spell those words correctly is also crucial. Accurate spelling helps to convey competence and professionalism.

Importance of Prefixes and Suffixes

The most common spelling mistakes are made when a **root word** (or a basic, core word) is modified by adding a prefix or a suffix to it. A **prefix** is a group of letters added to the beginning of a word, and a **suffix** is a group of letters added to the end of a word.

The prefixes usually change the meaning of the word. They might be negative or positive and signal time, location, or number. Note the spelling of the root word (or base word) does not change when adding a prefix.

Common Prefixes

Prefix	Meaning	Example
dis-	not, opposite	disagree, disproportionate
en-, em-	to make, to cause	encode, embrace
in-, im-	in, into	induct
ir-, il-, im-	not, opposite	impossible, irresponsible
mis-	bad, wrongly	misfire, mistake
mono-	alone, one	monologue
non-	not, opposite	nonsense
over-	more than, too much	overlook
pre-	before	precede
post-	after	postmortem
re-	again, back	review
un-	not, opposite	unacceptable

A suffix can change the base word in two ways:

- Change numerical agreement: turns a singular word into a plural word (a singular witness becomes plural witnesses)

- Change grammatical function: turns one part of speech into another (noun to verb, verb to adverb), such as moderation, moderating, or moderately

Common Suffixes

Suffix	Meaning/Use	Example
-able, -ible	able to	unbearable, plausible
-ance	state of being	significance
-al, -ial	relating to	lethal, testimonial, criminal
-ceed, -sede, -cede	go, go forward, withdraw, yield	exceed, recede, supersede
-ed	changes root word to past tense or past participle	called, played
-en	makes root word a verb	heighten, liven
-er	more, action, a person who does an action	clearer, sever, believer
-ful	full of	hateful, beautiful
-ian, -ite	person who does the action, part of a group	politician, meteorite
-ice, -ize	cause, treat, become	service, popularize
-ing	action	writing, playing
-ion, -tion	action or condition	celebration, organization
-ism	forms nouns referring to beliefs or behavior	Buddhism, recidivism
-ity, -ty	state of being	adversity, cruelty
-ive, -tive	state or quality	defensive, conservative
-less	without	tactless, nameless
-ly	in such a manner	poorly, happily

Common Suffixes		
Suffix	**Meaning/Use**	**Example**
-ment	action	endorsement, disagreement
-ness	makes root word a noun referring to a state of being	weakness, kindness
-or	a person who does an action	moderator, perpetrator
-s, -es	makes root word plural	weights, boxes
-sion	state of being	admission, immersion
-y	made up of	moody, greasy

Doubling-Up Consonants (or Not)

When adding some suffixes (usually, *-ing*, *-sion*) to a root word that ends in one vowel followed immediately by one consonant, *double that last consonant*.

Base Word	**Vowel/consonant**	**Suffix**	**Spelling Change**
wrap	a, p	-ing	wrapping
canvas	a, s		canvassing
admit	i, t	-sion	admission

This rule does not apply to multi-vowel words, such as *sleep*, *treat*, and *appear*. When attaching a suffix that begins with a vowel to a word with a multi-letter vowel followed by a consonant, *do not double the consonant.*

Base Word	**Multi-vowel, consonant**	**Suffix**	**Spelling**
sleep	ee, p	-ing	sleeping
treat	ea, t	-ed	treated
appear	ea, r	-ance	appearance

Do *not* double the consonant if the root word already ends in a double consonant or the letter *x* (examples—*add/adding, fox/foxes*).

Words Ending with *y* or *c*

If a root word ends in a single vowel *y*, the *y* should be changed to i when adding any suffix, unless that suffix begins with the letter *i*. If a root word ends in a two-letter vowel, such as *oy, ay,* or *ey*, the *y* is kept.

Root Word	**Ending**	**Suffix**	**Spelling Change**
baby	y	-ed	babied
stymy	y		stymied
crony	y	-ism	cronyism
say	y	-ing	saying
annoy	oy	-ance	annoyance
survey	ey	-ing	surveying

In cases where the root word is a verb (ending with the letter *c*) and the suffix begins with an *e, i,* or *y*, the letter *k* is added to the end of the word between the last letter and the suffix.

31

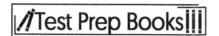

Root Word	Ending	Suffix	Spelling Change
panic	ic	-ing -y	panicking panicky
traffic	ic	-ed -er	trafficked trafficker

Words with *ie* or *ei*

There's an old saying "*I* before *E*, except after *C*." There's also a second part to it:

I before *E*,

Except after *C*,

Or when sounded as *A*,

As in *neighbor* and *weigh*.

Here are a few examples:

- *friend,* wield, yield (i before e)
- receipt, deceive (except after c)
- weight, freight (or when sounded as *a*)

Words Ending in *e*

Generally, the *e* at the end of English words is silent or not pronounced (e.g., *bake*).

- If the suffix being added to a root word begins with a consonant, keep the e.
- If the suffix begins with a vowel, the final silent e is dropped.

Root Word	Ending	Suffix	Spelling Change
waste remorse pause	silent *e*	-ful -s	wasteful remorseful pauses
reserve pause	silent *e*	-ation -ing	reservation pausing

Exceptions: When the root word ends in *ce* or *ge* and the suffix *–able* or *–ous* is being added, the silent final *e* is kept (e.g., *courageous, noticeable*).

Words Ending with *-ise* or *-ize*

Sometimes, it can be difficult to tell whether a word (usually a verb) should end in *–ise* or *–ize*. In American English, only a few words end with *–ise*. A few examples are *advertise, advise,* and *compromise*. Most words are more likely to end in *–ize*. A few examples are *accessorize, authorize, capitalize,* and *legalize*.

Words Ending with *-ceed, -sede,* or *-cede*

It can also be difficult to tell whether a word should end in *–ceed, –sede,* or *–cede*. In the English language, there are only three words that end with *–ceed: exceed, proceed,* and *succeed*. There is only one word that ends with *–sede: supersede*.

If a word other than *supersede* ends in a suffix that sounds like *–sede,* it should probably be *–cede.* For example: *concede, recede,* and *precede.*

Words Ending in *–able* or *–ible*

In the English language, more words end in *–able* than in *–ible:*

- e.g., probable, actionable, approachable, traceable
- e.g., accessible, admissible, plausible

Words Ending in *-ance* or *-ence*

The suffixes *-ance* and *-ence* are added to verbs to change them into nouns or adjectives that refer to a state of being. For example, when *-ance* is added to the verb *perform*, *performance* is formed, referring to the act of performing.

Suffix	When to use	Example
-ance, -ancy, -ant	<ul><li>When the root word ends in a *c* that sounds like *k*</li><li>When the root word ends in a hard *g*</li></ul>	<ul><li>significance</li><li>arrogance</li><li>vacancy</li><li>extravagant</li></ul>
-ence, -ency, -ent	<ul><li>When the root word ends in a *c* that sounds like *s*</li><li>When the root word ends in a *g* that sounds like *j*</li></ul>	<ul><li>adolescence</li><li>convergence</li><li>contingency</li><li>convergent</li></ul>

Words Ending in *-tion, -sion,* or *-cian*

The suffixes *–tion* and *–sion* are used when forming nouns that refer to the result of a verb. For example, the result of to *abbreviate* something is an *abbreviation.* Likewise, if a person has *compressed* something, then there is a *compression.*

The suffix *–cian* is used when referring to a person who practices something specific. For example, the person who practices *politics* is a *politician.*

Words Containing *-ai* or *-ia*

Unfortunately, there isn't an easy-to-remember rhyme for deciding whether a word containing the vowels *a* and *i* should be spelled *ai* or *ia.* In this case, it's helpful to rely on pronunciation to determine the correct spelling.

The combination of *ai* is one sound, as in the words capt*ai*n and f*ai*nt.

The combination of *ia,* on the other hand, is two separate sounds, as in the words guard*ia*n and d*ia*bolical.

It's helpful to say the word out loud to decide which combination of the two vowels is correct.

Rules for Plural Nouns

Nouns Ending in *-ch, -sh, -s, -x,* or *-z*
When modifying a noun that ends in *ch, sh, s, x,* or *z* to its plural form, add *es* instead of the singular *s*. For example, *trench* becomes *trenches, ash* becomes *ashes, business* becomes *businesses, jukebox* becomes *jukeboxes,* and *fox* becomes *foxes.*

This rule also applies to family names. For example, the Finch family becomes the *Finches,* and the Martinez family becomes the *Martinezes.*

Nouns Ending in *y* or *ay, ey, iy, oy,* or *uy*
When forming plurals with nouns ending in the consonant *y,* the *y* is replaced with *-ies.* For example, *spy* becomes *spies,* and *city* becomes *cities.*

If a noun ends with a vowel before a *y,* the *y* is kept, and an *s* is added. For example, *key* becomes *keys,* and *foray* becomes *forays.*

Nouns Ending in *f* or *fe*
When forming plurals with nouns ending in *f* or *fe,* the *f* is replaced with *v,* and *es* is added. For example, *half* becomes *halves,* and *knife* becomes *knives.*

Some exceptions are *roof/roofs* and *reef/reefs.*

Nouns Ending in *o*
When forming plurals with nouns ending in a consonant and *o,* the *o* is kept and an *es* is added. For example, *tomato* becomes *tomatoes.*

Musical terms are the exception to this rule. Words like *soprano* and *piano* are pluralized by adding *s* even though they end in a consonant and *o* (*sopranos, pianos*).

When forming plurals with nouns ending in a vowel and *o,* the *o* is kept, and *s* is added. For example, *ratio* becomes *ratios,* and *patio* becomes *patios.*

Exceptions to the Rules of Plurals

For some nouns, instead of changing or adding letters at the end of the word, changes to the vowels *within* the words are necessary. For example:

- *man* becomes *men*
- woman becomes women
- child becomes *children*

Some nouns, when pluralized, change entirely:

- *tooth* becomes teeth
- foot becomes feet
- mouse becomes *mice*

The opposite is also true; some nouns are the same in the plural as they are in the singular form. For example, *deer, species, fish,* and *sheep* are all plural nouns in singular form.

34

Vocabulary

Vocabulary is simply the words a person uses and understands on a daily basis. Having a good vocabulary is important in both written and verbal communications. Many of these materials may contain unfamiliar words, so it's important for officers to learn ways to uncover a word's meaning so they can use it correctly in their own writing.

To understand the challenges of using vocabulary correctly, imagine suddenly being thrust into a foreign country. Not knowing the right words to use when asking for basic necessities (e.g., food, a place to stay, a bathroom) would make everyday life extremely difficult. Asking for help from foreigners who don't share the same vocabulary is hard, since language is what facilitates understanding between people. The more vocabulary words a person understands, the more precisely they can communicate their intentions. This section of the study guide focuses on understanding and deciphering vocabulary through basic grammar.

Prefixes and Suffixes

In the previous section, we went over the particular *spelling* of prefixes and suffixes, and how they changed the root word. In this section, we will look at the *meaning* of various prefixes and suffixes when added to a root word. As mentioned before, a **prefix** is a combination of letters found at the beginning of a word, while a **suffix** is a combination of letters found at the end. A **root word** is the word that comes after the prefix, before the suffix, or between them both. Sometimes a root word can stand on its own without either a prefix or a suffix. More simply put:

> Prefix + Root Word = Word
>
> Root Word + Suffix = Word
>
> Prefix + Root Word + Suffix = Word
>
> Root Word = Word

Knowing the definitions of common prefixes and suffixes can help when trying to determine the meaning of an unknown word. In addition, knowing prefixes can help in determining the number of things, the negative of something, or the time and space of an object. Understanding suffix definitions can help when trying to determine the meaning of an adjective, noun, or verb.

The following charts review some of the most common prefixes, what they mean, and how they're used to decipher a word's meaning:

Number and Quantity Prefixes

Prefix	Definition	Example
bi-	two	bicycle, bilateral
mono-	one, single	monopoly, monotone
poly-	many	polygamy, polygon
semi-	half, partly	semiannual, semicircle
uni-	one	unicycle, universal

Here's an example of a number prefix:

The countries signed a *bilateral* agreement; both had to abide by the contract.

Look at the word *bilateral*. If the root word (*lateral*) is unfamiliar, the prefix (*bi-*) can provide a vital clue to its meaning. The prefix *bi-* means *two*, which shows that the agreement involves two of something, most likely the two countries, since *both had to abide by the contract*. This is correct since *bilateral* actually means "involving two parties, usually countries."

Negative Prefixes

Prefix	Definition	Example
a-	without, lack of	amoral, atypical
in-	not, opposing	inability, inverted
non-	not	nonexistent, nonstop
un-	not, reverse	unable, unspoken

Here's an example of a negative prefix:

The patient's *inability* to speak made the doctor wonder what was wrong.

Look at the word *inability*. In the chart above, the prefix *in-* means *not* or *opposing*. By replacing the prefix with *not* and placing it in front of the root word of *ability* (*able*), the meaning of the word becomes clear: *not able*. Therefore, the patient was *not able* to speak.

Time and Space Prefixes

Prefix	Definition	Example
a-	in, on, of, up, to	aloof, associate
ab-	from, away, off	abstract, absent
ad-	to, towards	adept, adjacent
ante-	before, previous	antebellum, antenna
anti-	against, opposing	anticipate, antisocial
cata-	down, away, thoroughly	catacomb, catalogue
circum-	around	circumstance, circumvent
com-	with, together, very	combine, compel
contra-	against, opposing	contraband, contrast
de-	from	decrease, descend
dia-	through, across, apart	diagram, dialect
dis-	away, off, down, not	disregard, disrespect
epi-	upon	epidemic, epiphany
ex-	out	example, exit
hypo-	under, beneath	hypoallergenic, hypothermia
inter-	among, between	intermediate, international
intra-	within	intrapersonal, intravenous
ob-	against, opposing	obtain, obscure
per-	through	permanent, persist

Prefix	Definition	Example
peri-	around	periodontal, periphery
post-	after, following	postdate, postoperative
pre-	before, previous	precede, premeditate
pro-	forward, in place of	program, propel
retro-	back, backward	retroactive, retrofit
sub-	under, beneath	submarine, substantial
super-	above, extra	superior, supersede
trans-	across, beyond, over	transform, transmit
ultra-	beyond, excessively	ultraclean, ultralight

Here's an example of a space prefix:

> The teacher's motivational speech helped *propel* her students toward greater academic achievement.

Look at the word *propel*. The prefix *pro-* means *forward* or *in place of* which indicates something relevant to time and space. *Propel* means to drive or move in a direction (usually forward), so knowing the prefix *pro-* helps interpret that the students are moving forward *toward greater academic achievement*.

Miscellaneous Prefixes

Prefix	Definition	Example
belli-	war, warlike	bellied, belligerent
bene-	well, good	benediction, beneficial
equi-	equal	equidistant, equinox
for-	away, off, from	forbidden, forsaken
fore-	previous	forecast, forebode
homo-	same, equal	homogeneous, homonym
hyper-	excessive, over	hyperextend, hyperactive
in-	in, into	insignificant, invasive
magn-	large	magnetic, magnificent
mal-	bad, poorly, not	maladapted, malnourished
mis-	bad, poorly, not	misplace, misguide
mor-	death	mortal, morgue
neo-	new	neoclassical, neonatal
omni-	all, everywhere	omnipotent, omnipresent
ortho-	right, straight	orthodontist, orthopedic
over-	above	overload, overstock,
pan-	all, entire	panacea, pander
para-	beside, beyond	paradigm, parameter
phil-	love, like	philanthropy, philosophic
prim-	first, early	primal, primer
re-	backward, again	reload, regress
sym-	with, together	symmetry, symbolize
vis-	to see	visual, visibility

Here's another prefix example:

The computer was *primitive*; it still had a floppy disk drive!

The word *primitive* has the prefix *prim-* which indicates being *first* or *early*. *Primitive* means the historical development of something. Therefore, the sentence infers that the computer is an older model because it no longer has a floppy disk drive.

The charts that follow review some of the most common suffixes and include examples of how they're used to determine the meaning of a word. Remember, suffixes are added to the *end* of a root word:

Adjective Suffixes

Suffix	Definition	Example
-able (-ible)	capable of being	teachable, accessible
-esque	in the style of, like	humoresque, statuesque
-ful	filled with, marked by	helpful, deceitful
-ic	having, containing	manic, elastic
-ish	suggesting, like	malnourish, tarnish
-less	lacking, without	worthless, fearless
-ous	marked by, given to	generous, previous

Here's an example of an adjective suffix:

The live model looked so *statuesque* in the window display; she didn't even move!

Look at the word *statuesque*. The suffix *-esque* means *in the style of* or *like*. If something is *statuesque*, it's *in the style of a statue* or *like a statue*. In this sentence, the model looks *like* a statue.

Noun Suffixes

Suffix	Definition	Example
-acy	state, condition	literacy, legacy
-ance	act, condition, fact	distance, importance
-ard	one that does	leotard, billiard
-ation	action, state, result	legislation, condemnation
-dom	state, rank, condition	freedom, kingdom
-er (-or)	office, action	commuter, spectator
-ess	feminine	caress, princess
-hood	state, condition	childhood, livelihood
-ion	action, result, state	communion, position
-ism	act, manner, doctrine	capitalism, patriotism
-ist	worker, follower	stylist, activist
-ity (-ty)	state, quality, condition	community, dirty
-ment	result, action	empowerment, segment
-ness	quality, state	fitness, rudeness
-ship	position	censorship, leadership
-sion (-tion)	state, result	tension, transition
-th	act, state, quality	twentieth, wealth
-tude	quality, state, result	attitude, latitude

38

Look at the following example of a noun suffix:

The *spectator* cheered when his favorite soccer team scored a goal.

Look at the word *spectator*. The suffix *-or* means *action*. In this sentence, the *action* is to *spectate* (watch something), thus a *spectator* is someone involved in watching something.

Verb Suffixes

Suffix	Definition	Example
-ate	having, showing	facilitate, integrate
-en	cause to be, become	frozen, written
-fy	make, cause to have	modify, rectify
-ize	cause to be, treat with	realize, sanitize

Here's an example of a verb suffix:

The preschool had to *sanitize* the toys every Tuesday and Thursday.

In the word *sanitize*, the suffix *-ize* means *cause to be* or *treat with*. By adding the suffix *-ize* to the root word *sanitary*, the meaning of the word becomes active: *cause to be sanitary*.

Context Clues

It's common to encounter unfamiliar words in written communication. When faced with an unknown word, there are certain "tricks" that can be used to uncover its meaning. **Context clues** are words or phrases within a sentence or paragraph that provide hints about a word and its definition. For example, if an unfamiliar word is anchored to a noun with other attached words as clues, these can help decipher the word's meaning. Consider the following example:

After the treatment, Grandma's natural rosy cheeks looked *wan* and ghostlike.

The unfamiliar word is *wan.* The first clue to its meaning is in the phrase *After the treatment,* which implies that something happened after a procedure (possibly medical). A second clue is the word *rosy,* which describes Grandma's natural cheek color that changed after the treatment. Finally, the word *ghostlike* infers that Grandma's cheeks now look white. By using the context clues in the sentence, the meaning of the word *wan* (which means *pale*) can be deciphered.

Below are some additional ways to use context clues to uncover the meaning of an unknown word:

Contrasts

Look for context clues that *contrast* the unknown word. When reading a sentence with an unfamiliar word, look for a contrasting or opposing word or idea. Here's an example:

Since Mary didn't cite her research sources, she lost significant points for *plagiarizing* the content of her report.

In this sentence, **plagiarizing** is the unfamiliar word. Notice that when Mary *didn't cite her research sources,* it resulted in her losing points for *plagiarizing the content of her report.* These contrasting ideas

infer that Mary did something wrong with the content. This makes sense because the definition of *plagiarizing* is "taking the work of someone else and passing it off as your own."

Contrasts often use words like *but, however, although,* or phrases like *on the other hand.* For example:

The *gargantuan* television won't fit in my car, but it will cover the entire wall in the den.

The unfamiliar word is *gargantuan*. Notice that the television is too big to fit in a car, <u>but *it will cover the entire wall in the den*</u>. This infers that the television is extremely large, which is correct, since the word *gargantuan* means "enormous."

Synonyms

Another method is to brainstorm possible synonyms for the unknown word. **Synonyms** are words with the same or similar meanings (e.g., *strong* and *sturdy*). To do this, substitute synonyms one at a time, reading the sentence after each to see if the meaning is clear. By replacing an unknown word with a known one, it may be possible to uncover its meaning. For example:

Gary's clothes were *saturated* after he fell into the swimming pool.

In this sentence, the word *saturated* is unknown. To brainstorm synonyms for *saturated*, think about what happens to Gary's clothes after falling into the swimming pool. They'd be *soaked* or *wet*, both of which turn out to be good synonyms to try since the actual meaning of *saturated* is "thoroughly soaked."

Antonyms

Sometimes sentences contain words or phrases that oppose each other. Opposite words are known as **antonyms** (e.g., *hot* and *cold*). For example:

Although Mark seemed *tranquil*, you could tell he was actually nervous as he paced up and down the hall.

The unknown word here is *tranquil*. The sentence says that Mark was in fact not *tranquil* but was instead *actually nervous*. The opposite of the word *nervous* is *calm*, which is the meaning of the word *tranquil*.

Explanations or Descriptions

Explanations or descriptions of other things in the sentence can also provide clues to an unfamiliar word. Take the following example:

Golden Retrievers, Great Danes, and Pugs are the top three *breeds* competing in the dog show.

If the word *breeds* is unknown, look at the sentence for an explanation or description that provides a clue. The subjects (*Golden Retrievers, Great Danes,* and *Pugs*) describe different types of dogs. This description helps uncover the meaning of the word *breeds* which is "a particular type or group of animals."

Inferences

Sometimes there are clues to an unknown word that infer or suggest its meaning. These **inferences** can be found either within the sentence where the word appears or in a sentence that precedes or follows it. Look at the following example:

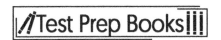
The *wretched* old lady was kicked out of the restaurant. She was so mean and nasty to the waiter!

Here the word *wretched* is unknown. The first sentence states that the *old lady was kicked out of the restaurant*, but it doesn't say why. The sentence that follows tells us why: *She was so mean and nasty to the waiter!* This infers that the old lady was *kicked out* because she was *so mean and nasty* or, in other words, *wretched*.

When preparing for a vocabulary test, try reading challenging materials to learn new words. If a word on the test is unfamiliar, look for prefixes and suffixes to help uncover what the word means and eliminate incorrect answers. If two answers both seem right, determine if there are any differences between them and then select the word that best fits. Context clues in the sentence or paragraph can also help to uncover the meaning of an unknown word. By learning new vocabulary words, a person can expand their knowledge base and improve the quality and effectiveness of their written communications.

Practice Quiz

For the first three questions, choose the word that is spelled correctly.

1. I'm _____ looking forward to my vacation this year.
    a. definitly
    b. definitely
    c. defenitely
    d. definately

2. I hope that scientists are able to prove the _____ of aliens.
    a. existanse
    b. esixtinse
    c. existense
    d. existence

3. The vehicle had a _____ problem that prevented it from starting.
    a. mechanical
    b. mecanical
    c. mekanical
    d. meckanical

For the next two questions, choose the synonym for the underlined word.

4. The city's first responders must follow <u>protocol</u> when handling calls for cases of domestic violence.
    a. Guidelines
    b. Internist
    c. Requests
    d. Evidence

5. After the riot broke out, officers had to use strong measures to <u>quell</u> the angry crowd.
    a. Wave
    b. Count
    c. Incite
    d. Calm

See answers on the next page.

Answer Explanations

1. B

2. D

3. A

4. A: *Guidelines* and *protocol* can be used as synonyms.

Guidelines: a set of standards created for a future action

Protocol: official guidelines or procedures that must be followed

5. D: *Calm* and *quell* can be used as synonyms.

Calm: to make tranquil or serene

Quell: to calm, quiet, or put an end to something

43

Memorization

The Memory section assesses a candidate's observational skills and his or her ability to recall facts and information. This is a very important skill that officers must employ daily during routine job duties.

On the exam, this section is typically composed of a couple of drawings or photographs that are followed by a series of multiple-choice questions. The questions are not viewable until the image is removed. Test takers examine each graphic one at a time, and then the image is removed. During the observation period, it is recommended that test takers study the image as carefully as possible, first examining the overall scene and then studying it more closely to identify and memorize details.

The questions that follow pertain to details from the graphic and must be completed from memory. Access to review the image again is not permitted. Because the questions pertaining to the image may address the picture on a general level as well as specific details, both elements need to be examined. For example, test takers may encounter an image of a prison cell containing several inmates who are fighting. One question may address the image as a whole, such as: "*what is the general mood of the image?*" Answer choices may be options such as *triumphant, hopeful, agitated*, and *peaceful.* In this case, *agitated* is the best choice. The majority of the questions will be about more specific details from the image. For example, questions for this same image may ask how many inmates were present in the scene, what time was displayed on the wall clock, what was the position of the cell door, or how many bars were running vertically on the window.

There are a variety of strategies that candidates employ to improve their scores in this section. Most test takers start by examining the entire image for a few seconds and then moving from this broad view to an increasingly specific study. Some people find that it works best to examine the picture in quadrants or in designated sections individually in a predetermined order to ensure that the entire image is studied without leaving gaps. Other candidates employ a variety of strategies depending on the particular image. For example, they may study the people first and then the environment surrounding the scene for an outdoor picture or start by looking at the walls and then the middle of the room indoors.

Other test takers start by trying to identify context clues from the scene, such as the sun position or weather in outdoor scenes or the clock time indoors to determine the season or time of day. Then, they may move on to try to count specific figures or subjects in the scene and identify distinguishing characteristics between such figures. For example, are there a different number of males and females present? Is someone wearing a distinguishing piece of clothing such as a hat? Exam questions often address things such as the time, place, and setting of the graphic. Others ask test takers to recall the number of certain items present, or to answer questions about a specific item in the image, which can be better answered if distinguishing features of the items are noted during the study period.

It is recommended that test takers practice with a variety of images and strategies to familiarize themselves with the process and to identify those methods that work best. A sample graphic similar to those that may be encountered on the exam is provided below. Test takers should study the graphic for two minutes and then completely remove it from their view while attempting the practice questions. Test takers can practice this section an unlimited number of times with the help of a partner or friend. The partner can find any type of image and generate a few questions about it and then pass it to the test candidate to attempt.

Interpreting Visual Depictions of Traffic Incidents

In cases in which traffic patterns are involved, it is important for an officer to be able to identify where traffic incidents have occurred. Different visual representations may be used online and physically to depict these situations. An officer needs to be able to interpret this data in its different forms in order to decide where the event occurred and the best course of action to take.

It is important to look for descriptions that detail how the visual data is represented for a given traffic incident depiction. The officer should look for areas of the depiction where symbols are described or defined as well as instructional text that may detail how the information is to be interpreted. Then, once the layout of the data is clear to the officer, the visual depiction can be scanned to locate the traffic incident and the surrounding area. Different visual depictions may need to be used to identify a specific problem. In this case, the officer should look for the information that relates to the incident and gather all the data needed to completely understand the situation and be up to date on any recent changes in traffic patterns.

Recognizing and Identifying Facial Features

Being an officer requires keen observational skills and careful attention to detail to identify and interpret important information when it comes to solving a case. In the instance of identifying potential culprits, the officer will need to pay close attention to the features of individuals who may be involved in the incident. Sketch artists help officers by rendering images of suspects based on spoken, visual descriptions. They will then create a sketch of what the person potentially looks like, making sure the sketch is as accurate as possible so that it is identifiable to others. However, an officer will often still have to look through numerous sketches to identify a specific person. To be able to accomplish this task and pick the most accurate drawing, the officer needs to have a strong memory of the individual particulars that make up the person they are matching with the sketch.

When identifying facial features, an officer should focus on specific details that stand out. Things that may appear more pronounced in the individual than on other faces should be taken note of as well as body modifications such as tattoos and piercings. These will help distinguish the individual from others when asked to identify them later on. However, trying to keep track of too much information may be confusing when it comes time to recall a specific face; therefore, to be sure their memory is correct, an officer should focus on the details that are the easiest to remember. They should also keep in mind that drawings will never be exact and they are searching only for the closest similarity, not the one that perfectly matches the face remembered. If an officer is having trouble recalling features or is stuck between similar options, the best choice will be the one with the most specific remembered features to match any verbal descriptions that may have been used to describe the individual to the artist.

Visualizing and Identifying Patterns and Objects

To compile the most resources available to an officer for solving cases, large amounts of data need to be collected and recorded. It will be the officer's job to interpret this data to reach accurate conclusions, turning scattered information into a more coherent case that can be visualized and interpreted. A lot of sensory data will need to be kept track of and deciphered to give the most objective description of an incident. Visual data will need to be recalled in order for situations to be recreated and utilized. The best way to organize this visual data when recalling an incident is to identify patterns and specific objects.

Important information in a case will often be repeated in different ways by different people. Identifying correlating data will help determine the veracity of the information because it can be confirmed by multiple sources and noted as patterns. For example, multiple witnesses may give different information about how tall a suspect may be but each mention that the suspect had a more noticeable trait such as long hair. Another example is if each party involved agrees to the time of a car accident. When the officer starts gaining additional information and identifying more patterns that are important objects involved in a case, they can better visualize the instance to help determine the best course of action to take. Visualizations of events help an officer organize and structure an incident to examine all possible conclusions.

Recalling Information from Wanted Posters

Wanted posters are used to relay information about individuals involved in open cases. It is important for an officer to familiarize themselves with different types of wanted posters so they can identify important information that may need to be recalled later to solve a case. The more information the officer is able to take mental note of, the better equipped they will be to find and identify a wanted person. It is unreasonable to assume that all the information written on a wanted poster will be memorized by an officer, especially if multiple wanted posters are involved; however, an officer is expected to know enough about the case to recall the key details needed when the wanted poster is not available.

To know what information is the most significant to focus on, it is first important to identify how the information on the wanted poster is laid out. Most people may think of the Old West when they think about wanted posters, with bold letters identifying the criminal and the crimes committed as well as a large picture of the wanted person in the center. Wanted posters as they appear now are actually relatively unchanged from what they used to be, formatted in the same way to convey the most important information as quickly as possible.

First, the officer should study the face of the individual on the poster enough to be able to recall it and then take note of the specific information, such as height, weight, and eye color, to be able to form and visualize an image of the way the complete person may appear. Once the officer is able to form a mental picture of the culprit based on the image and the description, they can then focus on the specific crimes committed in order to relate the facts of the case; these can usually be found in a text-based description surrounding the photo. Once a few of the most specific details are memorized, the officer can go to the next wanted poster and repeat the process until they can recall each individual in their mind without referring to the posters.

Finding the Perpetrator from a Description

When someone is arrested, information about their appearance and the crime or crimes they are being accused of is recorded. If the suspect in a case is still unknown, officers will most likely arrest multiple people. It is then the officer's job to determine which suspect is the culprit based on descriptions and information about those who have been arrested. Information provided to the officer may be in the form of a sketch or image, but often an officer will have to interpret written or spoken words used to describe the perpetrator. The officer will need to know how to best use this information to form an image of what the perpetrator may look like and to choose the corresponding person from a group of arrested suspects.

When processing information about an arrested person, the officer needs to first identify the key details that describe how the perpetrator may look. It is important to focus on descriptions that are unique and, if possible, character defining, that may help single the individual out from a group of similar-looking individuals. An officer should be careful of general descriptions, such as "tall" or "old," that are imprecise and can be relative to the individual who gave the information and focus on descriptions that can be easily visually recognizable. The officer should be able to form a detailed mental image of what they believe the culprit looks like based on the descriptions given. Then, when presented with those arrested, the officer can use this mental image to match which person they believe to be the perpetrator. However, an officer should never guess; if no arrests match the descriptions or lack distinctive details given about the perpetrator, more information will need to be gathered before a final decision should be made.

Identifying Meaningful Details

A scenario can involve a web of different and often conflicting sets of details. It is important for an officer to be able to identify the most and least meaningful details of a police scenario in order to focus on the information that will be the most helpful to solving a case. Although it is important to take note of as many details as possible when first encountering a case, in the long run, too many details for a given scenario will cause confusion if they are not vetted and organized. Focusing on finding the most and least meaningful details divides the information into what is the most relevant to the situation and what is superfluous to the case as a whole.

To discover which details are the most meaningful, it is important to first focus on the objective facts of the case. An officer should determine the beginning, middle, and end of the event; look for details that can be verified, such as time of day or objects involved; and value the information that is the most irrefutable, such as pictures or video of a scene. The credibility of each source should also be researched; the most credible information will be free from frequent changes of thought or details and will be the most understandable or logical in relation to the scenario.

The most meaningful details will also be frequently repeated, appearing in more than one source. The officer should determine what the frame of mind may have been like for those involved and how that might affect the information they have given. The least meaningful details in a police scenario will be the lies. It is important for the officer to spot where the untruthful information is and identify why it does not correlate with other data examined. Details that have no relation to the people or objects involved in the case are not very meaningful and should be set aside when organizing data into a complete case, whereas the most important details should be made to stand out.

Filling in Police Forms

Police forms are used by officers to organize information in a set way that can be easily interpreted by anyone who comes into contact with the information. This is done to set a standard behind all information reported for consistency of documentation. Forms will contain details related to an incident and will be used as a way to relay information about a case internally between parties. A police officer needs to be familiar with what these forms look like and the protocol for filling in blank reports or answering questions from a filled-in form. This way, they are able to not only file their own forms but to read and interpret the forms filled out by another officer.

Most information regarding an incident that is not directly witnessed will come to an officer in the form of a written incident description. It will then be the officer's job to use this written description to fill out a blank police department form. The form will help lay the information out in a way that others in the police department have been trained to interpret. There will be separate sections pertaining to different details of an event or crime. An officer should look at the headings of the forms to determine what information to provide for each section, being as detailed as possible without providing too much unimportant information.

The written description should not simply be copied over to the police form. The officer will need to interpret which data is the most important and how this data can be used to solve the case. Then, the officer will have to be able to read these forms to answer questions about an incident. Details should be able to be quickly spotted with the form because they will be laid out in a familiar way. Once the officer has familiarized themselves with the layout of the form, they can easily go to the specific section that contains the data needed to answer a question.

Practice Quiz

Directions:

Examine the image below for two minutes then remove it from view. Answer the questions that follow the image without referring back to the image. Do not read the questions during the image review period.

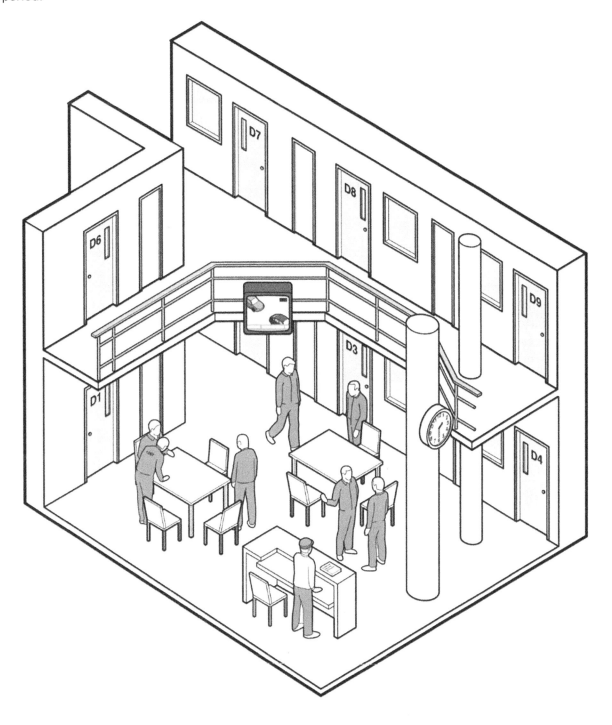

49

1. How many doors are located on the second floor?
    a. 1
    b. 2
    c. 3
    d. 4

2. How many inmates are located at the table on the left?
    a. 3
    b. 4
    c. 5
    d. 6

3. What time is it?
    a. 7:50
    b. 2:30
    c. 12:10
    d. 4:00

4. What is written on the right most door downstairs?
    a. D4
    b. D9
    c. C9
    d. C4

5. What was on the television?
    a. Animals
    b. A cartoon
    c. Planes
    d. The news

See answers on the next page.

Answer Explanations

1. D

2. A

3. B

4. A

5. D

Inductive Reasoning

Inductive and Deductive Reasoning

Generally speaking, there are two main types of reasoning—deductive and inductive. An inference based on **deductive reasoning** considers a principle that is generally believed to be true and then applies it to a specific situation ("All English majors love reading. Annabelle is an English major. Therefore, I can infer that Annabelle loves reading."). **Inductive reasoning** makes an inference by using specific evidence to make a general inference ("Trina, Arnold, and Uchenna are all from Florida. Trina, Arnold, and Uchenna all love to swim. Therefore, I can infer that people from Florida usually love swimming."). Both deductive and inductive reasoning use what is *known* to be true to make a logical guess about what is *probably* true.

As readers are presented with new information, they should organize it, make sense of it, and reflect on what they learned from the text. Readers draw conclusions at the end of a text by bringing together all of the details, descriptions, facts, and/or opinions presented by the author and asking, "What did I gain from reading this text? How have my ideas or emotions changed? What was the author's overall purpose for writing?" In this case, a **conclusion** is a unifying idea or final thought about the text that the reader can form after they are done reading. As discussed, sometimes writers are very explicit in stating what conclusions should be drawn from a text and what readers are meant to have learned. However, more often than not, writers simply present descriptions or information and then leave it up to readers to draw their own conclusions. As with making inferences, though, readers always need to base their conclusions on textual evidence rather than simply guessing or making random statements.

> When the school district's uniform policy was first introduced fifteen years ago, parents and students alike were incredibly enthusiastic about it. Some of the most appealing arguments in favor of enforcing school uniforms was to create an equal learning environment for all students, to eliminate the focus on fashion and appearance, and to simplify students' morning routine by removing the need to pick a different outfit every day. However, despite this promising beginning, the uniform policy has steadily lost favor over the years. First of all, schools did not notice a significant drop in examples of bullying at school, and students continue to report that they feel judged on their appearance based on things like weight and hairstyle. This seems to indicate that uniforms have not been particularly effective at removing the social pressure that teens feel to appear a certain way in front of their peers. Also, many parents have complained that the school's required uniform pieces like jackets, sweaters, and neckties can only be purchased from one specific clothing shop. Because this retailer has cornered the market on school uniforms, they are operating under a total monopoly, and disgruntled parents feel that they are being grossly overcharged for school clothing for their children. The uniform policy is set to be debated at the upcoming school board meeting, and many expect it to be overturned.

After reading this article, a reader might conclude any of the following: that ideas that start with popular support might become unpopular over time; or that there are several compelling counterarguments to the benefits of school uniforms; or that this school district is open to new ideas but also open to criticism. While each conclusion is slightly different, they are all based on information and evidence from the article, and therefore all are plausible. Each conclusion sums up what the reader learned from the passage and what overall idea the writer seems to be communicating.

52

Another way for readers to make sense of information in a text is to make **generalizations**. This is somewhat related to the concept of inductive reasoning, by which readers move from specific evidence to a more general idea. When readers generalize, they take the specific content of a text and apply it to a larger context or to a different situation. Let's make a generalization from the topic, the bystander effect:

> A bystander is simply a person who watches something happen. Paradoxically, the more people who witness an accident happen, the less likely each individual is to actually intervene and offer assistance. This is known as the bystander effect. Psychologists attribute the bystander effect to something called "diffusion of responsibility." If one individual witnesses an accident, that single person feels the whole burden of responsibility to respond to the accident. However, if there are many witnesses, each person feels that responsibility has been divided amongst many people, so their individual sense of responsibility is much lower and they are less likely to offer help.

This article describes one very specific psychological phenomenon known as the "bystander effect." However, based on this specific information, a reader could form a more general psychological statement such as, "Humans sometimes behave differently when they are alone and when they are in a group."

How to Approach Inductive Reasoning Questions

Questions that test inductive reasoning have several overlaps with deductive reasoning questions. This overlap occurs both in the question's structure and in its content. An inductive reasoning question is often prefaced with a passage providing information that you are expected to use when answering the test questions. More complex sections of the exam will ask multiple questions about a single preceding passage, with each question testing a different topic. Consequently, an important skill for solving inductive reasoning questions is the ability to distinguish them from deductive reasoning questions. Knowing which topic is being tested by a question makes the information needed to answer correctly easier to discern.

An inductive reasoning question typically provides *specific* information, rather than a widely encompassing procedure or generalization. The question then requires performing one of the following inductive tasks:

- Use many pieces of *specific* information to determine a general principle.
- Use the specific information to come to a *specific* conclusion.

Deductive and inductive questions often look similar because they ask you to perform similar mental tasks. The quickest way to recognize the difference based on a passage is to determine if the passage contains specific or general information. Drawing on the boxes analogy used when describing deductive reasoning questions, a passage testing your inductive reasoning generally provides objects rather than boxes. Skipping over the passage to read the questions is often helpful. Reading the question first helps the test taker determine which type of information they need to find in the passage, and determine which inductive task they are being asked to perform.

A **generalizing** question asks you to determine which answer provides the most reasonable abstraction or principle using the given information. You are being asked to choose the box into which the objects best fit. For example, if the passage lists twelve different crimes and their severity in terms of first,

second, or third degree, a generalizing question would ask for the principle that organizes these disparate crimes. You are being asked, for example, to generalize that a first-degree crime is more serious because it causes more harm.

A **concluding** question is structurally similar to questions of application. Instead of applying general principles to a specific situation, the test-taker is asked to reach a conclusion based on multiple pieces of specific information. One common type of passage that uses this type of question is collections of witness testimony. This often includes two to three sentences per hypothetical witness and is very dense with information about times, places, sights, and so on. This type of passage is an example of when jumping to the question is helpful. A question about time allows you to, for the most part, ignore non-time pieces of information in the passage. By finding similarities and differences in the witness statements, the test-taker is expected to choose the answer with a reasonable specific conclusion. For example, if four witnesses report seeing a red car at 1 PM and the fifth reports seeing it at 2:30 PM, it is reasonable to conclude the car left the crime scene around 1 PM.

Here are two example Inductive Reasoning questions:

Example 1. There has been a drive-by shooting on 8th Street. According to the four witnesses, the shooter was a white male in the passenger seat wearing a red sweatshirt, and the person driving the vehicle was wearing a black sweatshirt. The car was blue, with one rusty wheel well. The witnesses disagree on the vehicle's license plate number. Which of the following is most likely to be correct?
   a. BXD-4259
   b. BXO-4729
   c. 8XD-4229
   d. BXO-4229

Example 1. D: The answer to this question is Choice *D*, BXO-4229. Most of the information in this question is misleading and can be safely ignored because it does not help the test taker determine which plate is most likely correct. In this case, seeing that the question's answer choices are all letter-number combinations helps identify that the description of the crime is a distraction. This type of question is answered through comparing the information in each answer choice to determine the most probable answer. For example, Choice *C* begins with "8," while the other three answers begin with "B." Thus, the first character is most likely to be "B." However, it's important that you don't *exclude* Choice *C* from your consideration of the question entirely. Choice *C* isn't the correct answer, but its later characters can help determine the correct choice. The plate's third character doesn't provide additional information. Its fifth is likely "2," meaning that Choice *B* is incorrect. Its sixth is likely "2" as well, meaning that Choice *A* is incorrect. By process of elimination, we can conclude that Choice *D* is the correct answer.

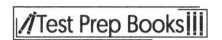

Example 2. Officer Ryan is looking over his patrol area's crime reports.

> Most stolen goods are sold between 10:00 p.m. and 2:00 a.m., most drug deals occur between 10:00 p.m. and 2:00 a.m., and most muggings occur between 9:00 p.m. and midnight.

> Most illegal goods are sold on Fridays, most drug deals occur on Saturdays, and most muggings occur on Saturdays.

> Illegal goods are reported to be sold between Cherry Avenue and Missouri Avenue, drug deals occur in the Conant Gardens neighborhood, and muggings occur by the dollar store off Interstate 40.

Officer Ryan will have the best chance of decreasing muggings if he patrols which of the following?
   a. The Conant Gardens neighborhood on Saturdays from 9:00 p.m. to 3:00 a.m.
   b. The dollar store off Interstate 40 on Saturdays from 8:00 p.m. to 1:00 a.m.
   c. Between Cherry Avenue and Missouri Avenue on Saturdays from 8:00 p.m. to 1:00 a.m.
   d. Between Cherry Avenue and Missouri Avenue from 9:00 p.m. to 3:00 a.m.

Example 2. B: This question is regarding only muggings, which, according to the data given, occur by the dollar store off Interstate 40 on Saturdays between 9:00 p.m. and midnight. The remaining choices, although the time or day may be correct, do not list the correct area according to the report.

Practice Quiz

1. Following a traffic accident, one of the vehicles drove away from the scene of the incident without waiting for police to arrive. Several witnesses gave a license plate number in addition to a description of the car. Which of the following plates is most likely to be correct?
   a. RTY-449I
   b. RYT-A491
   c. RYT-4401
   d. RYT-4491

2. The NYPD rewards individuals who report graffiti in progress to the police with $500.00 if their report results in the vandal's arrest. Which of the following is a reasonable conclusion based on this information?
   a. The city government values the cleanliness of the urban environment.
   b. The police department rarely catches individuals who create graffiti.
   c. The police department values increasing its number of arrests.
   d. The city government values punishing those who graffiti above rewarding informants.

Use the following information to answer questions 3-5.

> The NYPD uses a 3-level system to classify investigative encounters with members of the public. These levels rely upon the officer's suspicion of criminal activity.
>
> - Level 1 encounters occur when an officer requests information from a member of the public. The officer must have an objectively credible reason to approach the person and may not ask accusatory questions. The person may leave at any time without suspicion.
> - Level 2 encounters occur when the officer has found suspicion of criminal activity and is exercising their right of inquiry. The officer may ask accusatory questions and may ask for consent to search. The person may refuse to answer questions and is free to leave.
> - Level 3 encounters occur when a reasonable person would not feel free to walk away from the officer. The officer must have individualized reasonable suspicion of current or imminent criminal activity on the basis of facts (for example, seeing a person hurry away from the sound of a store's alarm). The officer may ask accusatory questions, may detain the person while investigating if there is probable cause for an arrest, and may ask consent to search. The officer may frisk the person if they reasonably suspect the person is armed and dangerous.

3. Which of the following is a reasonable definition of "founded suspicion" when initiating an investigative encounter?
   a. The officer suspects criminal activity based on the person's conduct or on reliable hearsay.
   b. The officer knows specific facts which leads them to believe that a crime has been, is being, or is about to be committed.
   c. The officer suspects the person is carrying a weapon and has intent to use it in conjunction with a crime.
   d. The officer has found evidence of illegal activity in the person's residence or vehicle.

56

4. Why might "stop" often be used as an alternative name for a level 3 encounter?
   a. The officer has stopped the civilian to ask them a question.
   b. The officer is permitted to detain the civilian temporarily.
   c. The encounter's purpose is to stop a crime in progress.
   d. The officer must refrain from using accusatory questions.

5. Which of the following is a reasonable conclusion about the 3-level system of investigative encounters?
   a. Level 1 encounters occur any time an officer interacts with a civilian.
   b. Pulling over a speeding vehicle is a common type of level 2 encounter.
   c. Higher level encounters are more likely to result in an arrest.
   d. Level 1 encounters only occur when investigating a misdemeanor.

See answers on the next page.

Answer Explanations

1. D: Choice *D* is correct because the license plate given uses the most frequent character for each position in the answer. Choices *A, B,* and *C* are incorrect because each answer has at least one aberrant character.

2. A: Choice *A* is correct because the reward is an incentive that works toward increased cleanliness in the city. Choice *B* is incorrect because the existence of a reward does not necessarily indicate that arrests of those who graffiti are low. Choice *C* is incorrect because a single piece of information does not entail such a broad conclusion about the NYPD's values. Choice *D* is incorrect because information about graffiti fines has not been provided to compare with the informant reward.

3. A: According to the NYPD, "founded suspicion" occurs when a person's behavior seems suspicious, or when the officer has received reliable hearsay that the person may have been involved in criminal activity. Choice *B* is incorrect because the passage indicates that specific facts provide reasonable suspicion, not founded suspicion. Choices *C* and *D* are incorrect because each answer is an example of a specific fact that would justify a level 3 encounter. Thus, Choice *A* must be correct.

4. B: During a level 3 encounter, the officer is permitted to temporarily detain a person. This is not permitted in level 1 and level 2 encounters. Thus, Choice *B* is correct because it describes a characteristic of a level 3 encounter that is reasonably associated with the name "stop." Choices *A* and *C* are incorrect because they are true of all three encounter types. Choice *D* is incorrect because during a level 3 encounter the officer is permitted to use accusatory questions.

5. C: Choice *C* is correct because a level 3 encounter permits detaining the person while determining if the officer has probable cause for an arrest. Level 1 and 2 encounters prioritize seeking information and are less likely to end in an arrest. Choice *A* is incorrect because not all officer-civilian interactions are investigative. Choice *B* is incorrect because pulling over a vehicle is often a level 3 encounter, due to the temporary detainment of the driver while their identification and registration is confirmed. Choice *D* is incorrect because a level 1 encounter might occur with any severity of crime.

Deductive Reasoning

Deductive reasoning involves starting with stating a general rule, and then moving forward with logic to obtain a desired conclusion. If the original statements are true, then the conclusion is true.

Questions on this exam which test your deductive reasoning generally begin with a passage, procedure, or other mode of descriptive text. This passage provides the principle or principles that the tester is expected to apply to information in the test question and its answers. Your task is to apply the *general* to the *specific* and produce the correct conclusion. It's important to remember that while the content of these passages refers to specialist information (such as NYPD operating procedure), the exam does not test your knowledge—it tests your ability to deduce. All information needed for the question is available in the passage.

Some common deductive tasks required by the exam include identifying specific information that **conforms** or **contrasts** with the passage and finding the relevant piece of general information to **apply** to a specific situation.

Spotting the correct answer to this type of question requires you to conceive of each general piece of information as if it were the label for a box of objects The purpose of each question is to determine if each answer option fits inside or outside of that box. A conforming-type question will ask which of the answers fits inside the box, and a contrasting-type question will ask which does not. For example, if the passage provides information about legal consequences for juvenile offenders, then those consequences would only apply to persons under the age of 18. An answer specifying the offender is 16 conforms, while an answer specifying the offender is 19 does not.

More complex questions of this nature increase the amount of information in the passage, or specify additional boxes with which the answer ought to conform or contrast. When working with an especially long—or conceptually dense—passage it can be helpful to leap forward to the associated questions. Then, return to the passage and seek the applicable principles. For example, if the passage provides a 7-step procedure for how and when to break down a door, it can be useful to first determine which element of the task is sought by the associated question.

Another useful technique for solving these questions is to identify a significant word or phrase, and then skim for that signifier in the passage. For example, if a question asks about situations in which an officer should report "10-84" to dispatch, it is useful to skim the passage for instances of "10-84." This winnows down the amount of information you need to handle to answer the question.

This technique is sometimes useful as well with questions applying the passage to a situation. However, the difference between application and conform/contrast questions is that the specific situation often does not correlate as easily or obviously with the passage's general information. For example, a question which describes the crime scene when an officer arrives may then ask which action is correct to perform next. This requires the tester to deduce the action from the procedure associated with the passage. Questions of application often require understanding the sequence of events required by a procedure, and then understanding conditional statements (if... then...) which guide officer decisions. Unlike information ordering questions, deduction questions typically require *using* a sequence, rather than *producing* a sequence.

Example

1. According to New York law, elder abuse occurs when a crime is committed by a caregiver that victimizes a vulnerable elderly person. A vulnerable elderly person is defined as someone over the age of sixty who suffers from infirmity associated with advanced age, and the infirmity makes the person unable to mentally, emotionally, or physically care for themselves. Which of the following crimes constitutes elder abuse?

    a. A forty-five-year-old woman strikes a sixty-six-year-old man on the shoulder with an open hand, leaving a bruise.

    b. A sixty-two-year-old man with stage 4 dementia complains that his caregiver hasn't driven him to a dental appointment.

    c. A seventy-two-year-old woman who lives with two unrelated women is stabbed by her housemate.

    d. A fifty-four-year-old woman who cannot walk due to severe arthritis is prevented from leaving her apartment by her son, who lives with her.

1. B: Choice *B* is correct because the victim is over the age of sixty, and the abuser is a caregiver. With this question, the first step is to identify victims who are over the age of sixty. Doing so eliminates Choice *D*. The second step is to determine which of the remaining choices includes an abuser who is a caregiver. Choices *A* and *C* do not describe the abuser's relationship as one providing care to the victim. Therefore, Choice *B* is the answer which fits into the box provided by the question.

Practice Quiz

1. One definition of second-degree manslaughter in New York is recklessly causing the death of another person. In which of the following situations has the criminal committed second-degree manslaughter?
   a. A driver going seven miles over the speed limit collides with the front passenger door of another vehicle. The person in that vehicle's passenger seat suffers laceration of their carotid artery and is declared dead at the hospital.
   b. A woman swings a rolling pin at her wife during an argument. The strike knocks the victim down a flight of stairs, and the victim breaks her neck. The victim dies before emergency services arrive.
   c. An electrician is doing work for her former husband and installs a faulty fuse in his house with the intent of causing a fire and damaging the house. During the fire, the man's paraplegic aunt dies from asphyxiation.
   d. An employer instructs their employee to use a plastic safety shield while operating a power saw. Later in the day, the employee continues using the saw without a shield. The employee's hand is severed, and the employee dies from blood loss and shock.

Use the following information to answer questions 2-3:

The following is true about modern license plates on passenger vehicles licensed in the state of New York:

- Passenger plates begin with three letters, then show the state symbol, and end with four numbers.
- Passenger vehicles are required to have a front and a rear license plate.
- No vehicle without a license plate may be operated, driven, or parked on public roads.
- License plates shall be kept clean and uncovered so that they are readable.

2. Which of the following vehicles is most likely to be violating New York law?
   a. A school bus on a residential street with the license plate 24109-BB in front and back
   b. A minivan on the interstate with the Pennsylvania license plate BUS-1972 in back and a Phillies baseball plate in front
   c. A sedan parked on the lawn with no license plate in back
   d. An SUV with the license plate FFI-4592 in front and a muddy license plate in back

3. Which of the following combinations of front and rear plates most likely licenses a vehicle from New York?
   a. Front: B2B-972A; Rear: B2B-972A
   b. Front: BIY-8842; Rear: BIY-8842
   c. Front: GHC-9970; Rear: GHC-9920
   d. Front: blank; Rear: XWS-1568

Use the following information to answer questions 4-5:

The maximum sentence of imprisonment for a misdemeanor or violation depends on the category of crime of which the individual has been convicted:

- Class A misdemeanors cannot be sentenced to more than 364 days imprisonment.
- Class B misdemeanors cannot be sentenced to more than ninety days imprisonment.
- Unclassified misdemeanors cannot be sentenced to more than 364 days imprisonment.
- Violations cannot be sentenced to more than fifteen days imprisonment.

4. Which of the following criminals has most likely committed a Class B misdemeanor?
    a. A nineteen-year-old woman convicted of self-abortion in the second degree and imprisoned for sixty-two days
    b. A twenty-four-year-old male police officer convicted of official misconduct and imprisoned for 300 days
    c. A seventeen-year-old male convicted of first-degree manslaughter and imprisoned for seven years
    d. A sixty-seven-year-old male convicted of trespassing and imprisoned for seven days

5. Based on the above information, which of the following statements is most likely true?
    a. Unclassified misdemeanors cause more harm than Class A misdemeanors.
    b. Violations occur infrequently in New York.
    c. Class A misdemeanors cause more harm than Class B misdemeanors.
    d. Class A misdemeanors are the most common class of criminal activity.

See answers on the next page.

Answer Explanations

1. A: Choice *A* is correct because the speeding driver was engaged in reckless behavior without the intent to harm another person. Choice *B* is incorrect because the criminal intended to harm her wife. Choice *C* is incorrect because the criminal intended to harm her ex-husband. Choice *D* is incorrect because the employee's reckless behavior resulted in their own death, not the death of another person.

2. D: Choice *D* is correct because the muddy license plate is a violation of New York law. Choice *A* is incorrect because a school bus is not a passenger vehicle. Choice *B* is incorrect because the vehicle is not from New York; not all states require both front and rear plates. Choice *C* is incorrect because the vehicle is not parked on a public road.

3. B: Choice *B* is correct because the plates have the correct format and are identical in front and back. Choice *A* is incorrect because the second character is a number, not a letter. Choice *C* is incorrect because the front and rear plates do not match. Choice *D* is incorrect because the front plate is blank.

4. A: Choice *A* is correct because the woman was imprisoned for more than fifteen days and less than ninety days. Thus, it is likely that she was imprisoned for a Class B misdemeanor. Choices *B* and *C* are incorrect because the individual was imprisoned for longer than ninety days. Choice *D* is incorrect because the individual was imprisoned for less than fifteen days.

5. C: Choice *C* is correct because Class A misdemeanors have a longer maximum sentence than Class B misdemeanors. Consequently, it is reasonable to deduce that a Class A misdemeanor causes more harm to the public than Class B. Choice *A* is incorrect because Class A and unclassified misdemeanors have the same maximum sentence. Choices *B* and *D* are incorrect because the length of a sentence does not have a logical association with the frequency of that category of crime.

Information Ordering and Problem Sensitivity

Police officers are expected to determine a timeline when responding to call. This process involves taking witness statements, collecting information, and then compiling a logical sequence of events.

Ordering and Managing Facts Logically

Details for a case can build up quickly as new information comes in from different sources. Multiple people will also usually be involved in a case, making it important for an officer to be able to order and manage the facts from multiple accounts of an incident to reach the most informed conclusions. Data that has not been logically ordered is difficult to understand and may lead to confusion and an inability to find the true facts of a case. When the information is organized and presented in a way that is easier to follow, solutions to the problems are more identifiable because all the relevant details can be processed in a logical progression. When a case is just beginning, information will come to the officer in a disorganized way; it will be up to the officer to find all the facts of the case and reorganize them so they can be better used and understood. It is also important to have this logical progression of facts in order for others who may not have collected the data to be able to read about and understand the case at any moment.

Common instances of scrambled facts come in the form of witness statements. Several factors, such as the high emotional states of the witnesses, their lack of factual details, or the sheer number of witnesses involved, contribute to the sometimes disorganized data an officer receives. When obtaining information from a witness, an officer needs to first identify the facts of the case. True facts can be validated from multiple sources; they also are spoken with more confidence and relate to specific, objective details over emotional experiences. Once the officer has identified all the facts in an incident, they can then begin to place the facts in logical order. It is helpful for the officer to progress in a linear way, starting with what happened first and providing a progression of events up until the time of reporting. Once the facts follow a forward trajectory, they can be better used to recreate the scene and progress the information into a conclusion.

Problem Sensitivity

Problem Sensitivity assesses a candidate's critical thinking skills and his or her ability to identify and apply information to a problem or potential problem. This is a very important skill that officers must employ daily during routine job duties.

On the exam, some questions will supply you with information about certain policies or regulations, and a situation in which you will have to apply the information. Your job is to determine what the best course of action is for the given situation. Other questions will be centered around a scenario with various witness statements. All questions will be in multiple-choice format.

There are a variety of strategies that candidates employ to improve their scores in this section. Most test takers start by carefully examining all of the information provided, reading the question, and then reading the information again. This will help to educate you on the background information, consider the specific situation and formulate an opinion, and then verify if you are correct.

Other test takers find that it is easier to read the question before reading the information to save time. This strategy may be helpful to some, but it is not recommended because the questions are based

exclusively on the information provided. If you read the question before you read the information, you may choose the incorrect answer based on your outside knowledge of the subject.

Identifying the Most and Least Meaningful Details in a Police Scenario

A scenario can involve a web of different and often conflicting sets of details. It is important for an officer to be able to identify the most and least meaningful details of a police scenario in order to focus on the information that will be the most helpful to solving a case. Although it is important to take note of as many details as possible when first encountering a case, in the long run, too many details for a given scenario will cause confusion if they are not vetted and organized. Focusing on finding the most and least meaningful details divides the information into what is the most relevant to the situation and what is superfluous to the case as a whole.

To discover which details are the most meaningful, it is important to first focus on the objective facts of the case. An officer should determine the beginning, middle, and end of the event; look for details that can be verified, such as time of day or objects involved; and value the information that is the most irrefutable, such as pictures or video of a scene. The credibility of each source should also be researched; the most credible information will be free from frequent changes of thought or details and will be the most understandable or logical in relation to the scenario. The most meaningful details will also be frequently repeated, appearing in more than one source. The officer should determine what the frame of mind may have been like for those involved and how that might affect the information they have given.

The least meaningful details in a police scenario will be the lies. It is important for the officer to spot where the untruthful information is and identify why it does not correlate with other data examined. Details that have no relation to the people or objects involved in the case are not very meaningful and should be set aside when organizing data into a complete case, whereas the most important details should be made to stand out.

Finding the Most Appropriate Response to Police Scenarios

A police scenario can be any number of instances that are related to a case. An officer needs to be ready to make the most appropriate responses based on a combination of their training and reasoning abilities. An officer's actions should not only help to solve cases but should be made to first and foremost ensure the safety of those involved. Each police scenario will be different, so it may be difficult sometimes to decide what the correct course of action might be. Decisions also need to be made quickly in the event a scenario necessitates an immediate response. An officer will also be required to analyze and interpret data involved from multiple sources to fully understand other situations to make informed conclusions.

The first step to finding appropriate responses for a police scenario requires the collection and analyzation of data so the officer can be properly informed on the situation. The most useful data will be the honest facts, and therefore details will need to be researched to confirm the veracity of the data. If a more immediate action is needed, the officer will have to pay close attention to all the surrounding details and take note of anyone who is in immediate danger. Actions must be backed up based on the facts of the case later. After examining the details, an officer should think of several different actions that could be taken. These options should be contrasted with each other to determine which action

would best fit the situation. The final decision should be the one that most conforms to the law and is the safest course of action to prevent danger in the field.

Applying Police Policies

It is important for an officer to completely understand the written details of any case they may be working on. Police policies have been put in place to create a method for examining and interpreting data presented to an officer. When an officer applies these police policies, they have a better chance of completely comprehending the case and can make better use of the data presented. Having the most important details is not enough if the officer cannot understand and use these details to make the most informed decisions. An officer should read all the details of an incident to have a clear understanding of each case that is presented to them. Although there may not be an objectively right way to interpret data, when it comes to the law, the most accurate interpretation will be the one that most coincides with the written law. Police policies are the tools an officer will use to interpret information by this standard of the law.

To start applying police policies to given situations, an officer needs to have a clear understanding of the policies of their local office. The officer should study the law definitions and be able to relate incidents to specific crimes as they are defined in text. Having a clear understanding of the laws in their area is the first step to applying these policies to specific cases. Once a thorough understanding of the law has been established, an officer should read and reread each report of an incident brought to them until they can form as clear a picture of the scene as possible. Then, the officer can start to draw comparisons to what they have read about the law, and specific police policies can be applied to the situation.

Frequency of Information Questions

Some of the most useful information involved in a case will come directly from witnesses. However, not all witnesses will give completely accurate information that can be used to solve the crime. It will be up to the officer to determine what information is factual and which witnesses are giving the most accurate reports of the incident.

When determining which witness is giving the most factual details of a case, there are a few factors the officer can immediately determine, such as if the witness was actually there at the time of the crime or the amount of details a witness actually observed. If the witness was too far away to see anything important or if they were not directly involved in the case, their information will most likely not be worth much attention. An officer should also take into consideration how much time has passed between the crime and the questioning of the witness; if more time has elapsed, the information may not be remembered as clearly.

After the witness's relation to the scene of the crime is determined, the officer can then interpret the confidence and completeness of their responses to determine which is the most truthful. True statements will be made confidently and stated in a way that can be clearly understood. True information will also appear frequently in more than one witness's testimony. If details about a case are repeated in the same way by multiple witnesses, the officer knows the information is most likely true. The witness who is telling the truth will be the one who can be backed up by other sources of evidence as well. The officer should ask about key details they already know to be true to see how the witness responds. The witness who is the most truthful will be the one who can back up their story with factual data.

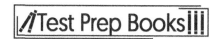

General Information Ordering

Information ordering is a category that tests your ability to work with **sequences.** Demonstrating the ability to sequence exercises the capacity to reason and extrapolate about different types of content. A famous example of numerical sequencing is the Fibonacci sequence:

$$1, 1, 2, 3, 5, 8, ...$$

The Fibonacci sequence follows the mathematical rule that the two previous numbers, added together, produce the next number in the sequence. For example, if a question asked, "What is the next number in the above sequence?" the correct answer would be 13.

Mathematical sequencing is not common on this exam. The Fibonacci sequence, however, is a useful example because it demonstrates the type of thinking required when practicing information ordering. Other types of ordering exercises you're already familiar with include determining an efficient route through a grocery store or figuring out when a past event happened based on other memories or details.

Chronology is an important aspect of information ordering because it demonstrates your ability to understand the logic of time. After all, a car with a dead battery can't start. If the car was started in the past, it therefore must have been started sometime before the battery died. The concepts of "before" and "after" can organize events into a necessary sequence.

Another important concept associated with information ordering is **hierarchy**. The use of hierarchy demonstrates an officer's ability to order objects, actions, values, and so on according to a correct sequence of priority, size, cost, and other factors. Where a chronological sequence *has* to occur in the given order, due to the nature of time, a hierarchical sequence is conceptually more fluid. Some hierarchies are straightforward (such as those using numbers), while others are vague (such as those structuring social status or moral values).

As the examples of hierarchy, chronology, and mathematics demonstrate, information ordering processes are generally organized using a standardized rule or principle. In a case like the Fibonacci sequence the rule is relatively simple (and you may even be asked to logically infer the rule from the given sequence). In other cases, the rules of a sequence are made complex through the addition of multiple steps and the use of **conditional** statements. A conditional statement follows an "if... then..." structure. Conditional statements create branches in a set of rules that require a particular branch to be followed if the appropriate condition is met.

How to Approach Information Ordering questions

In general, information ordering questions on this exam ask the prospective officer to **apply** a given set of rules to one or more situations. These situations reflect actual challenges an officer would experience while on duty. However, information ordering questions can require you to logically sequence any type of object—such as using a map to determine the best route to a destination—so it's important not to assume a question without an associated set of rules is not an information ordering question.

The rules used in these questions are drawn from the NYPD's operating procedures. They are often abbreviated or reflect just one section of the provided procedure. It's important to remember that

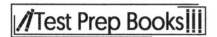
information ordering questions are *not* testing your knowledge of police procedure. Rather, they're testing your ability to analyze and use the information given during the exam.

Questions that begin with a passage describing a procedure are best handled by initially skipping the procedure and reading forward to the questions. Determine how you're intended to apply the procedure to the given situation. Then, return to the procedure and look for the relevant pieces of information. This process helps you analyze the passage more quickly and find information more accurately because it relies less on memory. It's generally easier to pinpoint specific information than it is to keep a whole passage present in your mind.

When you use this question-solving process, watch for conditional statements ("if... then..." statements) in the procedure. These statements create additional complexity because their rule is only required in specific situations. When it is not required, the test-taker is expected to move to the next section of the procedure. A conditional branch of a procedure may have several lines in the procedure's description. Especially complex questions may provide topics or incorrect choices that use information on an irrelevant branch. When these branches are presented in sequence, remember that the top of a conditional branch is the most important part of that section. If the beginning of a conditional is not relevant, actions described in later steps within that branch are likewise irrelevant.

Example

Use the following passage to answer question 1.

> When a police officer arrives at the scene of a traffic accident, they are expected to use the following procedure to guide their actions.

I. Radio dispatch to report their arrival.

II. Examine the scene and determine potential hazards to the officer's safety.

III. Determine if any civilians require medical attention.

   A. If a civilian is injured, radio dispatch to send an ambulance.

   B. Provide first aid to those most badly injured until paramedics arrive.

IV. Record license and registration information for all participants.

Example 1. An officer responds to a 911 call reporting an accident at Columbus Circle. When they arrive, both drivers are sitting beside their vehicles off the road. One is clutching their right elbow with their left hand and is shouting at the other driver. Their right hand is limp. Per the above procedure, what should the officer do next?
   a. Ask the civilian what's wrong with their right hand.
   b. Radio for an ambulance to be sent.
   c. Calm down the shouting civilian.
   d. Put up traffic cones to keep vehicles from coming near.

Example 1. B: This question is about sequencing the officer's actions based on the scene described. Choice *B* is correct because the officer sees an injury. Per the procedure, they should call for an

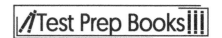

ambulance immediately—the officer does not require additional information before making the call. Thus, Choice *A* is incorrect. Choice *C* is incorrect because medical assistance is prioritized over de-escalation. Choice *D* is incorrect because the question indicates the vehicles are already off the road. The officer does not need to act on section (II) because there is not a current hazard.

Practice Quiz

1. Officer Mcleod was called to a college dorm, where a concerned student had reported that a batch of cocaine that was circulating at a frat party had been poisoned. Upon arriving at the party, the Officer spoke to several members of the fraternity, who swore they were not aware that the cocaine was poisoned and promised to assist the Officer in any way they could. After turning off the music and bringing up the lights, the Officer could see that certain individuals appeared to be heavily sedated or even in some stage of overdose. He was quickly able to assist and revive all the individuals, and many of them quickly became conscious and cognizant. One of them told Officer Mcleod they had acquired the cocaine from a fellow student at a library on campus, and a rumor quickly began to spread that the student was a disgruntled chemistry major. Officer Mcleod then headed over to the library to attempt to locate the student, on the advice of another student at the party, who claimed that student usually spent the whole night at the library on weekends. Upon arriving at the location where he was told the student dealt, Officer Mcleod found no one around, although the lights, which were on a thirty minute on/off toggle, were still on.

Who first informed Officer Mcleod that the student dealing the poisoned cocaine was a disgruntled chemistry student?
   a. The 911 operator who relayed the information from the student who made the original call.
   b. The members of the frat informed Officer Mcleod when he first arrived at the party.
   c. The security officer at the library informed Officer Mcleod when he arrived at the library to look for the student.
   d. No one in particular told Officer Mcleod; it arose as a rumor while Officer Mcleod was assisting students at the frat party.

2. A police officer should prioritize multiple injured civilians in order of most likely to least likely to result in death. Which of the following injuries has the HIGHEST priority?
   a. An amputated little finger on the right hand
   b. A third degree burn on the chest and left arm that exposes bone
   c. An unconscious, breathing civilian with no visible wounds
   d. A fractured shin that renders the civilian unable to walk

Use the following passage to answer questions 3-5:

At times, NYPD officers are expected to patrol the interior of residential buildings operated by the New York City Housing Authority. The following is an excerpt of the procedure describing that task.

   I. Notify dispatch of beginning of patrol using code 10-75I. Log the street address and the time.

   II. Inspect the exterior doors and door locks, intercom system, and lobby.

   III. Inspect elevators.

   A. If the elevators are inoperable, notify the Housing Authority.

   IV. Document if signs prohibiting trespassing are a) legible, and b) prominently displayed.

   A. If the signs are a) missing, b) illegible, or c) defaced, document with a Field Report.

70

V. Proceed to the top floor by elevator, if possible.

    A. Patrol the roof and landing.

    B. Patrol each staircase, floor, and hall from top floor to ground floor.

    C. Document malfunctions in a Field Report.

VI. Notify dispatch upon leaving the building. Log the time.

3. Which of the following spotted on an interior patrol requires a report to the Housing Authority?
    a. A defaced trespassing sign on the ground floor
    b. Torn carpet on third-floor landing
    c. A person sleeping in the second-floor hallway
    d. An out-of-order elevator on the fifth floor

4. When is an officer required to use their radio during an interior patrol?
    a. Upon completing each floor
    b. To report the code 10-75I
    c. When they reach the roof
    d. To report a missing sign

5. During an interior patrol, an officer notices the third floor "Residents Only" sign is covered in red and black ink graffiti. What should the officer do?
    a. Record the graffiti in their Field Report.
    b. Stop a nearby resident and ask for information.
    c. Seek soap and water to clean the sign.
    d. Contact dispatch to notify the NYCHA.

See answers on the next page.

Answer Explanation

1. D: First, organize the information and events from the passage in chronological order:

First, a concerned student reported to the police that a batch of cocaine that had been circulating at a party was poisoned.

In response, Officer Mcleod was dispatched to the dorm room where the frat party occurred. Upon arriving at the party, Officer Mcleod spoke to several members of the fraternity, who claimed they did not know what was going on and would assist however they could.

Upon turning on the lights and turning off the music, Officer Mcleod became aware that certain students seemed to be heavily sedated or even in some stage of overdose. Fortunately, Officer Mcleod was able to revive and assist all the affected individuals, who quickly became to wake up once more.

One of the students Officer Mcleod assisted then informed him that they had acquired the cocaine from a fellow student at a campus library, and soon the students began to claim that the individual was a disgruntled chemistry major. Another student then informed the Officer that the student was usually in the library the whole night on the weekends, and specifically told the Officer the location inside the library where the student dealt cocaine.

Upon arriving at the location in the school library, Officer Mcleod found on one around, but did notice that the lights, which were on a thirty minute on/off toggle, were still on.

Choice D is correct because Officer Mcleod first heard that the student dealing the poisoned cocaine was a disgruntled chemistry student while he was assisting students at the party, and it wasn't from one student in particular that the rumor first came. Choice A is incorrect because the original 911 contained no information about who poisoned the cocaine. Choice B is incorrect because the members of the frat did not know how poisoned the cocaine when Officer Mcleod first arrived. Choice C is incorrect because Officer Mcleod had already known about the rumor at that point, and furthermore he did not speak to any security officer there.

2. B: Choice B is correct because a bad burn across a significant portion of the civilian's body is most likely to cause death, especially if the burn is close to the heart. Choice A is incorrect because the amputation is less likely to cause death than the burn. Choice C is incorrect because the civilian is breathing and thus unlikely to be in danger of dying before they receive medical attention. Choice D is incorrect because the fracture is not described as putting the person's life at risk.

3. D: Choice D is correct because it can logically be concluded from section (IIIA) that an inoperable elevator on any floor is reported to the Housing Authority, not to the police department. Choice A is incorrect because a defaced sign is reported with a Field Report. Choice B is incorrect because the excerpt does not require reporting this damage. Choice C is incorrect because the excerpt does not provide guidance on dealing with possible trespassers.

4. B: Choice B is correct because it can be inferred that information passed along immediately (such as a dispatch code) uses a rapid system of reporting (such as the radio), rather than a more formal method such as a Field Report or a Civil Summons. Choice A is incorrect because section (VB) does not require the officer to radio after patrolling each floor. Choice C is incorrect because section (V) does not direct the officer to report their arrival on the roof. Choice D is incorrect because a missing sign is recorded with a Field Report.

5. A: Choice *A* is correct because the graffiti renders the sign "illegible" and therefore should be documented per section (VC) of the preceding passage. Choices *B* and *C* are incorrect because the passage does not direct the officer to investigate incidents or to repair illegible signs. Choice *D* is incorrect because the officer is directed to contact the Housing Authority only if the elevator is inoperable.

Spatial Orientation

Reading Maps to Find the Quickest Route

An officer should be familiar with different types of visual maps so they can always know the quickest route to a specific location. Road maps, subway maps, traffic maps, bus routes, etc., should all be able to be read quickly regardless of the map's visual style. An officer will need to know how to use both online and physical maps and be able to direct themselves as well as others as to the best route to take at a given time.

Generally, the easiest way to interpret a map is to look for the map key. The key will contain all the information relating to what each symbol on the map means as well as the distance scale that determines how far areas are from each other. Some maps may have this information explained in text instead of in a separate key, so the officer will need to know where to find the information that explains how the map is to be used. Finding the quickest route then means knowing where the initial starting point is, analyzing the routes on the map, and identifying which route provides the shortest amount of travel time. It is important to remember that sometimes the shortest distance between two points is not the quickest route. Traffic patterns, stops, speed limits, or other restrictions could add more travel time depending on the route and should be taken into consideration when searching for the most efficient route.

How to Approach Spatial Orientation Questions

Questions testing spatial orientation focus on your ability to understand directions based on a provided map. The test taker does not need to know real-world circumstances—focus on what the test provides, rather than personal knowledge. Spatial orientation questions often come in the following categories:

- Following directions to a destination
- Selecting the correct directions

In a **following** question, the test taker is asked to determine where the directions lead from an origin. This might be a road intersection (such as Croyden and Berkshire) or a labeled landmark (such as Memorial Field).

In a **selecting** question, the test states the origin and the destination. Then, the test asks which directions provide the correct route. Often, none of the directions are "perfect." The test taker's task is to find flaws in the directions—such as turning right instead of left—to determine the best answer.

Physically manipulating the map helps answer both types of questions. Turning the map orients yourself correctly. Start oriented with **north** facing upward. Determine your origin, then use a finger or pencil to follow the question's directions. In a selecting-type question, you may need to do so multiple times to determine the correct answer. As you read the directions, keep in mind that most questions will vary the manner in which the directions describe the route. While turning the map, remember that compass directions are constant, while positional directions (such as left and right) are relative to your current position.

74

Some common difficulties to watch out for in spatial orientation questions include **deceptive** routes or **illegal** routes. These are most common in selecting-type questions because, by providing multiple sets of directions, the question has additional opportunities to mislead the test taker.

Deceptive routes are *almost* correct but make one important error that leaves the answer incorrect. For example, a question might indicate turning east off a road, but the turn is actually west. The question then proceeds as if it had said to turn west, leading to the destination. Consequently, it's important to follow routes carefully.

Illegal routes are just that—illegal. They indicate going the wrong direction on a one-way street, walking on an Interstate, or performing other actions generally proscribed by state law. All potential legal difficulties will be clearly marked on the provided map. For example, one-way streets will have an arrow indicating the street's direction. Illegal routes are always incorrect.

Example Spatial Orientation Question

The following map is used for this example question:

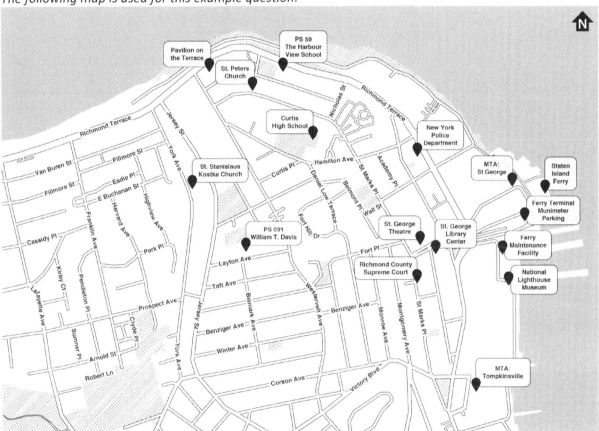

Example Question: You are driving south in a car starting at St. Stanislaus Kostka Church. Proceed southwest, and take the first right. Then, take the second right, and travel north to the third intersection. Turn left, and stop at the next intersection. Where are you?

a. Franklin Avenue and Eadie Place
b. East Buchanan Street and Franklin Avenue
c. PS 031 William T. Davis
d. Jersey Street and Richmond Terrace

Example Explanation. A: The correct answer in this example is Choice *A*. These directions lead you southwest along York Avenue until you take a right turn onto Prospect Avenue. Then, you make a right turn onto Franklin Avenue and a left turn onto the U-bend in the road, which returns to the intersection of Franklin Avenue and Eadie Place. Thus, Choice *A* is correct. Choice *B* makes the mistake of turning north on Harvard Avenue. Choices *C* and *D* make the mistake of turning left while on York Avenue, then trying to fit the rest of the directions to an incorrect portion of the map.

Practice Quiz

Use the following map for questions 1-5:

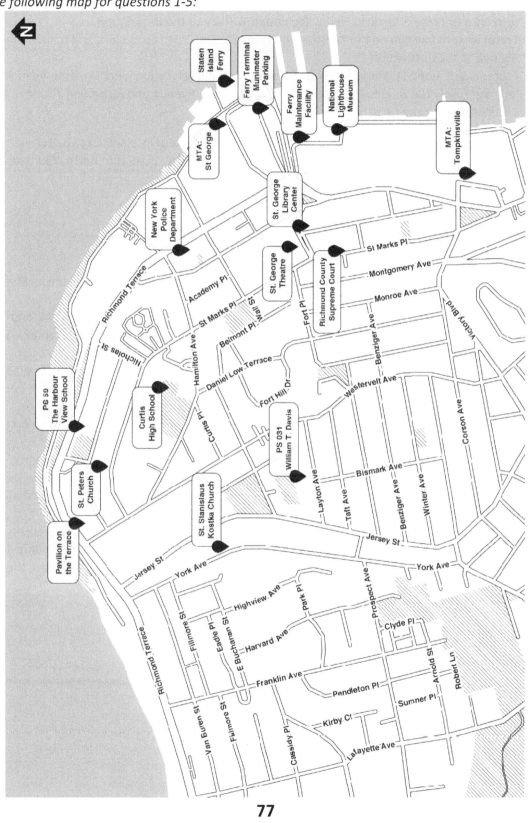

77

1. Which of the following is the best route from PS 59 The Harbour View School to the New York Police Department?
   a. Proceed east along Richmond Terrace until you reach the destination.
   b. Proceed east until you reach the intersection with Nicholas Street. Turn left, then make a right turn onto Richmond Terrace. Follow Richmond Terrace to the destination.
   c. Travel west to Pavilion on the Terrace, and turn left. Take the second left, and follow Hamilton Avenue to the destination.
   d. Proceed east along St. Marks Place until you reach the intersection with Hamilton Avenue. Turn left, and follow the road to the intersection of Hamilton Avenue and Richmond Terrace. Your destination is on the right.

2. You're walking east from Sumner Place on Arnold Street. At the third intersection, you turn left. You take the next turn east and proceed to the following intersection. Then, you turn north. You take the first left, then head south to the second intersection. Where are you?
   a. Arnold Street and Prospect Avenue
   b. Pendleton Place and Arnold Street
   c. Franklin Avenue and Arnold Street
   d. Robert Lane and Arnold Street

3. What is the shortest route from the National Lighthouse Museum to the corner of Franklin Street and Van Buren Street?
   a. Follow the road west to Richmond Terrace, and turn left. Proceed north along Richmond Terrace past Pavilion on the Terrace, then take a left turn on Franklin Avenue. The destination is at the first intersection.
   b. Follow the road west to Richmond Terrace. Turn right, then turn southwest at the intersection before the New York Police Department. Take a right onto St. Marks Place, then a left onto Hamilton Avenue. Follow Hamilton to Westervelt Avenue, and turn right. Take a left on Richmond Terrace, then turn south at the third intersection. The destination is at the first intersection.
   c. Travel south and follow the road west past MTA: Tompkinsville. Take the first turn north, then turn left onto Victory Boulevard. Follow Victory until you reach Jersey Street. Take the first left after Benziger Avenue, then cross York Avenue to Prospect Avenue. Turn north on Franklin Avenue, and proceed to Van Buren Street.
   d. Travel south and follow the road west past MTA: Tompkinsville. Take the first turn north, then proceed onto St. Marks Place. Follow St. Marks Place to Hamilton Avenue, and turn left. Take the third right, then make a right turn off Westervelt Avenue. Take the third left turn, then proceed south to Van Buren Street.

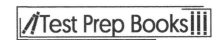

4. A person unfamiliar with the area asks you for directions. Which route from Ferry Terminal Munimeter Parking to St. Stanislaus Kostka Church is simplest?

    a. Travel west until you reach Richmond Terrace, then take a left. Follow the road until you reach Corson Avenue, and turn right. Proceed until you reach Jersey Street, and turn right. Take the second left, then continue north until you're at the church.

    b. Travel west to Richmond Terrace, and turn north. You'll go past the New York Police Department, PS 59 Harbour View School, and Pavilion on the Terrace. Take the seventh left after the police station, and go south until you see the church.

    c. Leave the terminal going west, and turn left onto Richmond Terrace. Take a right around the corner, then turn left past St. George Library Center. Turn right onto St. Marks Place, and follow the road to Hamilton Avenue. Take a left and go all the way to the end of the road. Turn left, then take the second left to get over to Jersey Street. The first left on Jersey will take you to York Avenue, then you just head north.

    d. Follow Richmond Terrace past the New York Police Department, then turn left onto Jersey Street. Loop back around north onto York Avenue, and the road goes straight to St. Stanislaus Kostka Church.

5. You start at the intersection of Richmond Terrace and Franklin Avenue and drive east. You take the third south turn, then take the first west. When you reach the T intersection, you head south and then take the first left turn. Which of the following landmarks are you closest to?

    a. Richmond County Supreme Court

    b. Pavilion on the Terrace

    c. St. George Theatre

    d. St. Stanislaus Kostka Church

See answers on the next page.

Answer Explanations

1. A: Choice *A* is correct because this route is direct and accurate. Choice *B* is incorrect because the map most likely indicates that PS 59 The Harbour View School is on Richmond Terrace, not the unlabeled street to the south. Choice *C* is incorrect because the second left would put the driver on St. Marks Place, not Hamilton Avenue. Choice *D* is incorrect because it begins from St. Peters Church.

2. C: Choice *C* is correct because the directions describe a loop of short streets that returns south along Franklin Avenue to Arnold Street. Choice *A* is incorrect because the route never reaches Prospect Avenue. Choice *B* is incorrect because this answer results from turning left at the second rather than the third intersection. Choice *D* is incorrect because the directions do not lead to that intersection.

3. B: Choice *B* is correct because it is the shortest route that is also correct. Choice *A* is incorrect because turning left on Richmond Terrace does not lead to the rest of the route. Choices *C* and *D* are incorrect because these routes cover a longer distance than Choice *B*.

4. A: Choice *A* is correct because this answer's directions are clearly described with left and right turns and use a minimal number of roads to provide simplicity. Choice *B* is incorrect because the directions' reliance on landmarks and counting turns is not simple. Choice *C* is incorrect because the directions require more turns than Choice *A*. Choice *D* is incorrect because the directions are vague about the distance from one landmark or street to the next.

5. D: Choice *D* is correct because, of the listed landmarks, this route leaves you closest to the church. The route ends on Layton Avenue, near PS 031 William T. Davis. However, that landmark is not among the answer choices provided. Choices *A*, *B*, and *C* are incorrect because each landmark is farther from Layton Avenue than St. Stanislaus Kostka Church.

Visualization

Officers must be able to visualize what suspects may look like with changes to their hair color or length, facial hair, and other indicators such as skin tone or tattoos. Visualizing what a suspect may look like with any of these changes helps officers identify them more easily.

On the exam, you will be given a photo of a suspect's face, and a short description of how he has altered his appearance. You will then have to identify him out of a lineup of four other suspects.

Identifying Patterns and Objects

To compile the most resources available to an officer for solving cases, large amounts of data need to be collected and recorded. It will be the officer's job to interpret this data to reach accurate conclusions, turning scattered information into a more coherent case that can be visualized and interpreted. A lot of sensory data will need to be kept track of and deciphered to give the most objective description of an incident. Visual data will need to be recalled in order for situations to be recreated and utilized. The best way to organize this visual data when recalling an incident is to identify patterns and specific objects. Important information in a case will often be repeated in different ways by different people.

Identifying correlating data will help determine the veracity of the information because it can be confirmed by multiple sources and noted as patterns. For example, multiple witnesses may give different information about how tall a suspect may be but each mention that the suspect had a more noticeable trait such as long hair. Another example is if each party involved agrees to the time of a car accident. When the officer starts gaining additional information and identifying more patterns that are important objects involved in a case, they can better visualize the instance to help determine the best course of action to take. Visualizations of events help an officer organize and structure an incident to examine all possible conclusions.

Recognizing and Identifying Facial Features

Being an officer requires keen observational skills and careful attention to detail to identify and interpret important information when it comes to solving a case. In the instance of identifying potential culprits, the officer will need to pay close attention to the features of individuals who may be involved in the incident. Sketch artists help officers by rendering images of suspects based on spoken, visual descriptions. They will then create a sketch of what the person potentially looks like, making sure the sketch is as accurate as possible so that it is identifiable to others. However, an officer will often still have to look through numerous sketches to identify a specific person. To be able to accomplish this task and pick the most accurate drawing, the officer needs to have a strong memory of the individual particulars that make up the person they are matching with the sketch.

When identifying facial features, an officer should focus on specific details that stand out. Things that may appear more pronounced in the individual than on other faces should be taken note of as well as body modifications such as tattoos and piercings. These will help distinguish the individual from others when asked to identify them later on. However, trying to keep track of too much information may be confusing when it comes time to recall a specific face; therefore, to be sure their memory is correct, an officer should focus on the details that are the easiest to remember. They should also keep in mind that drawings will never be exact and they are searching only for the closest similarity, not the one that

81

perfectly matches the face remembered. If an officer is having trouble recalling features or is stuck between similar options, the best choice will be the one with the most specific remembered features to match any verbal descriptions that may have been used to describe the individual to the artist.

How to approach Visualizing questions

Visualizing questions should be approached thoughtfully and intentionally. Each of these questions is followed by a diagram that presents four answer choices. The pictures included in the diagram only have slight differences from each other, making it easy to choose incorrectly. This is the nature of identifying suspects—sometimes there are only slight differences between the appearance of the person you are looking for and that of someone entirely uninvolved. There are a number of strategies that can be useful in approaching these questions.

First, it is essential to fully analyze the diagram offered with each question. Take quick notes on the tangible differences you notice. No feature is irrelevant, as even the smallest detail could be the difference between the correct and incorrect choices. Many applicants find that it can be useful to analyze the diagram before reading the question so that the features they are taking note of are not tainted by the details presented in the written question.

Next, taking one's time in the analysis of the question and corresponding answer choices is paramount. It can be tempting to instinctually choose the answer that one is first drawn to; however, that choice may be based on preconceived notions and the tendency to choose the first detail that sticks out. Questions are often designed with the intention of drawing one's eyes to details that may be irrelevant to the question at hand.

Lastly, strong time management skills and dedication to each question are essential. It is best to focus one's attention on one visualizing question at a time. Skipping ahead and looking through multiple visualizing questions can be detrimental, as details and features can start to merge, making it harder to accurately answer the question at hand. Knowing that each question will require concentrated focus, be aware of the time dedicated to each question in the context of the overall time limit.

Practice Quiz

1. The suspect is believed to be wearing a wig. Which of the following is the same person?

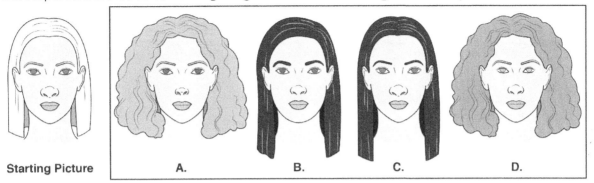

Starting Picture   A.   B.   C.   D.

2. The suspect is believed to have sustained some injuries to the face since his last sighting. Which of the following is the same person?

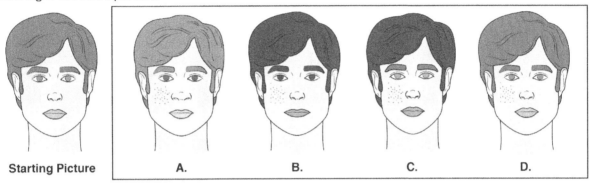

Starting Picture   A.   B.   C.   D.

3. The suspect is believed to have gained weight since her last sighting. Which of the following is the same person?

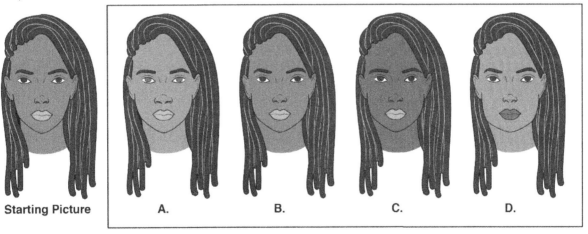

Starting Picture   A.   B.   C.   D.

Visualization

4. The suspect is believed to have grown out his hair. Which of the following is the same individual?

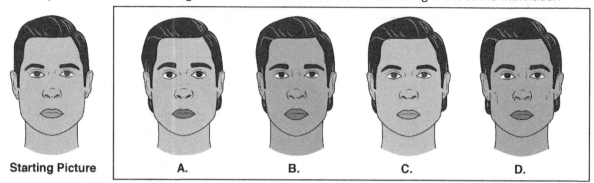

Starting Picture   A.   B.   C.   D.

5. The suspect is believed to have had surgery to alter her nose. Which of the following is the same person?

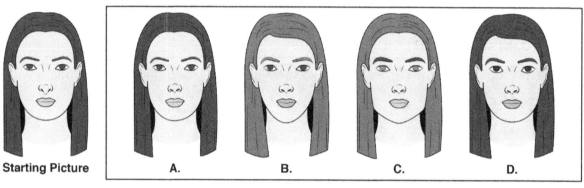

Starting Picture   A.   B.   C.   D.

See answers on the next page.

Answer Explanations

1. C: The correct answer is Choice *C*, as the facial features are the same; only the hair is different. Choice *A* is incorrect, as the face has a smaller, upturned nose. Choice *B* is incorrect, as the facial structure is fuller. Choice *D* is incorrect, as this individual's eyes are smaller and closer together.

2. D: The correct answer is Choice *D*, as it is the same face but with some scarring on the left cheek. Choice *A* is incorrect, as this individual has a wider nose. Choice *B* is incorrect, as this individual has more wide-set eyes. Choice *C* is incorrect, as this individual has narrower cheeks.

3. B: The correct answer is Choice *B*, as this is the same face but with fuller cheeks, which one might develop because of weight gain. Choice *A* is incorrect, as this individual has a larger nose. Choice *C* is incorrect, as this individual's eyes are more closely set together. Choice *D* is incorrect, as this individual has a square jawline.

4. C: The correct answer is Choice *C*, as this is the same face but with hair altered in length. Choice *A* is incorrect, as this individual has a different eye shape. Choice *B* is incorrect, as this individual has a narrower jawline. Choice *D* is incorrect, as this person has narrower cheeks.

5. A: The correct answer is Choice *A*, as this is the same face but with an altered nose. Choice *B* is incorrect because this person has an oval rather than rounded face. Choice *C* is incorrect, as this person's jawline is different. Choice *D* is incorrect, as this person's eyes are larger and rounder.

Written Comprehension

The next two questions are based on the following passage:

The majority of records that are taken as part of court proceedings are considered part of the public domain, and are therefore available to anyone who requests access. These documents can be used to conduct background checks, revealing information such as age, marital status, military status, and whether a person has ever been convicted of a crime. While many records are made public, some are sealed by a judge for extraordinary circumstances, such as to protect the privacy of a minor. Each state has its own rules governing which records can be accessed and counties determine how. In some cases the records can be obtained through a quick search of a state or county database, but others will require a request of the appropriate department. For example, in the state of California, most court records can be accessed through county court databases, but supreme and appellate court records are only available from the Appellate Court.

1. Based on the preceding passage, which of the following statements is most accurate?
   a. All court records can be accessed via online databases.
   b. Court records are always part of the public domain, so they can be accessed by anyone.
   c. Military status is private, so it cannot be revealed in court documents.
   d. For various reasons, some documents are sealed, so they are not accessible to the public.

2. Based on the preceding passage, which of the following statements is most accurate?
   a. Each state determines how and when court records can be accessed by the public.
   b. A judge should seal all court records for minors.
   c. A judge can seal a court record for any reason.
   d. California allows all court records to be accessed by county record databases.

The next two questions are based on the following passage:

Conducting a traffic stop can be one of the most dangerous parts of being a police officer. In light of the many traffic stop incidents that have occurred all over the country, many states are looking at how to address the problem. Recently, the state of Illinois passed a new law that adds traffic stop training to their driver's education courses. These courses are aimed to make new drivers prepared for all the possibilities of the road, and a potential traffic stop by a police officer is one of those possibilities. Proponents of traffic stop training say that this could help new drivers, especially young teens, not to panic in the event they get pulled over. If they know what to expect and how to handle a traffic stop, it is hoped that they could protect themselves from doing anything that could be perceived as a threat, such as reaching under the seat or arguing with the officer. As this new driver's education component gains popularity, it could be seen in more states across the US, and hopefully reduce the amount of traffic stop incidents.

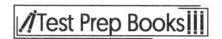

3. Based on the preceding passage, which of the following statements is most accurate?
   a. A new law in Illinois makes it required for all drivers to take driver's education courses.
   b. Lawmakers believe that traffic stop training will help police officers stop more underage drivers.
   c. Arguing with an officer is illegal during a traffic stop.
   d. The new law in Illinois adds traffic stop training to driver's education courses.

4. Based on the preceding passage, which of the following statements is most accurate?
   a. Traffic stops are not dangerous.
   b. Police officers can teach new drivers how to act when they are pulled over.
   c. Traffic stop training aims to protect young drivers from panicking when they are pulled over.
   d. Young drivers should not worry about being pulled over if they are driving safely.

The next two questions are based on the following passage:

> Federal law does not restrict the open carry of a weapon in public. Each state determines its own open carry laws. While there are some restrictions to these laws, such as having to gain a permit, or the prohibition of carrying a weapon in certain locations, such as a school or on public transportation, most states allow the open carry of a handgun. Currently, thirty-one states allow private citizens to open carry a firearm without a license. Only three states, California, Florida, and Illinois, and the District of Columbia, prohibit open carry of a firearm. Concealed carry refers to carrying a firearm under clothing or in a way that is not visible to the casual observer. Every state and the District of Columbia allow the concealed carry of a firearm in some form. Forty-two states do require a permit for concealed carry. Of these forty-two states, some have a "may issue" law that allows for wider denial of the permit and others have a "shall issue" law, which generally accepts most permits without discretion.

5. Based on the preceding passage, which of the following statements is most accurate?
   a. Open carry laws are strict in all fifty states.
   b. Only California, Florida, and Illinois allow for open carry of a firearm without a permit.
   c. Nineteen states require a permit for open carry of a firearm.
   d. Most states allow for open carry of a firearm with limited restrictions.

6. Based on the preceding passage, which of the following statements is most accurate?
   a. Eight states require a permit for concealed carry of a firearm in public.
   b. States that have a "may issue" law have very little restrictions on who can get a concealed carry permit.
   c. All states allow for the concealed carry of a firearm in public.
   d. States that have a "shall issue" law have strict restrictions on who can carry a weapon.

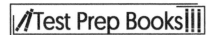

The next two questions are based on the following passage:

Since the 1966 Supreme Court case, Miranda v. Arizona, police officers have been required to read the Miranda rights, or Miranda warning, to any person taken into police custody. The Miranda rights include the following:

- You have the right to remain silent.
- Anything you say can and will be used against you in a court of law.
- You have the right to an attorney.
- If you cannot afford an attorney, one will be appointed for you.

To fully comply with Miranda rights, the person in custody must also waive their rights, typically in writing. If they do not waive their rights, any information they provide is not admissible in court. Police officers are required to read these rights so that the person in custody is aware of them, but also to protect the information that is given in any questioning they might conduct. When a person in custody is not Mirandized, anything they say, such as a confession, or the location of evidence, cannot be used in court.

7. Based on the preceding passage, which of the following statements is most accurate?
   a. The Miranda rights require the person in custody to remain silent.
   b. The Miranda rights are the result of a Supreme Court case.
   c. Police officers are not always required to read the Miranda rights to a person in custody.
   d. The Miranda rights tell the person in custody that they don't need a lawyer.

8. Based on the preceding passage, which of the following statements is most accurate?
   a. Miranda rights only protect the person in custody.
   b. Police officers who do not read Miranda rights to a person in custody can be sued.
   c. A person must waive their Miranda rights in order for the information they provide to be admissible in court.
   d. Any information gained from a person in custody who has not waived their Miranda rights can be used in court.

The next two questions are based on the following passage:

Many police departments have begun using social media outlets such as Twitter, Facebook, and Instagram to their benefit. Police departments have found that the use of social media can be very helpful in identifying suspects, alerting the community to a possible threat, locating a missing person, and even gaining support for their organization. Social media is a two-way street, so police departments are also able to get valuable information and feedback from the communities they serve. Departments who use social media report that when their community feels like they have a forum to voice their opinion, it creates a sense of trust in the police. Departments that do opt to use social media should abide by some simple rules such as limiting the amount of information released, especially on ongoing cases, using appropriate language, and having a single point of contact to manage the sites for continuity. Social media can be a great asset to any police department if used appropriately.

9. Based on the preceding passage, which of the following statements is most accurate?
   a. Police departments should make a Facebook page, but avoid Twitter and Instagram.
   b. Social media has been helpful to police departments in identifying suspects and locating missing persons.
   c. Community trust is not built through the use of social media outlets.
   d. Social media can be helpful to police departments, but it is not used very often.

10. Based on the preceding passage, which of the following statements is most accurate?
    a. Police departments should try to use a single person to manage social media pages.
    b. Police departments should make full use of social media by revealing the details of ongoing cases.
    c. Social media is not beneficial in ongoing cases.
    d. Police departments that want to use social media should hire a consultant to set up their sites.

The next two questions are based on the following passage:

When it comes to violent crime, one of the most important aspects of identifying and convicting a suspect is the collection of evidence. There are several steps in the process of collecting physical evidence including being able to identify what on or near a crime scene should and can be considered evidence. Crime scene investigators are trained in identifying latent prints; footwear and tire tracks; biological, drug, firearm, trace and digital evidence; and tool and tool mark evidence. Once evidence is identified, it must be collected, maintained, and stored in a way that ensures the integrity of the evidence. More specifically, investigators must wear gloves and change them as necessary to ensure there is no contamination, store items separately and in appropriate containers also avoiding cross-contamination, seal and initial the items with a date and time stamp, and then carefully monitor the chain of custody. Failure to adhere to the very stringent rules of evidence collection and storage can jeopardize the use of that evidence should the case come to trial.

11. Based on the preceding passage, which statement is most accurate?
    a. How evidence is stored is not as important as how it's collected.
    b. Avoiding cross-contamination is one of the most important elements of evidence collection.
    c. Crime scene investigators are ultimately responsible for a prosecutor's success in convicting a suspect.
    d. Collecting everything from a crime scene is a strategy used by crime scene investigators.

12. Handling evidence at a crime scene is an important process. It includes which step listed here:
    a. Identifying a suspect
    b. Avoiding cross-contamination
    c. Monitoring the chain of custody
    d. Wearing gloves

The next two questions are based on the following passage:

Eyewitnesses are essential to crime scene investigations. Not only can they help identify suspects, but their information may be useful in charging and convicting an individual as well. For that reason, how a law enforcement officer questions this individual is of the utmost importance. Because witnesses to crimes are human and how the human brain stores information is sometimes unreliable, procedures have been developed to ensure officers are

able to effectively collect and preserve eyewitness evidence. One of the first goals is that, when making first contact with the witness, the dispatcher should gather information from the witness in a way that is not suggestive or leading. Questions, throughout the entire evidence gathering process, should be open ended, allowing the witness to provide information as it comes to them. Follow-up questions may be more specific and ask for details based on initial answers. Therefore, they may be close ended. For example, if the witness says they saw a car, it is appropriate to ask what color or type of car they saw. In contrast, a leading or suggestive question might offer a color to the witness rather than waiting for them to answer, such as "Was it the car blue?" Additionally, to prevent contamination of eye witness evidence, officers responding to a scene should separate witness and make it clear that it's inappropriate for them to discuss what they saw.

13. Based on the above passage, why is it important to ask open ended questions?
    a. Open-ended questions allow you to ask follow-up questions.
    b. Open-ended questions are only effective if followed by a close ended question.
    c. Open-ended questions allow the witness to provide information without leading them.
    d. Open-ended questions allow you to lead the witness to useful information.

14. Based on the above passage, what should a responding officer do with witnesses?
    a. Suggest they discuss what they saw to create a full picture.
    b. Immediately gather information using open ended questions.
    c. Get their names and information and allow them to leave.
    d. Separate them to avoid contamination of the evidence.

The next three questions are based on the following passage:

Writing a police report may seem simple, but there is a big difference between writing a police report and writing a good police report. Above all, good reports are organized and clear. To write the best report possible, those two elements are paramount. Unfortunately, organization is often a challenge and when organization is non-linear, clarity can be lost as well. More specifically, when combining multiple stories from multiple people relaying what happened to them, what they witnessed, and even what the writer witnessed upon arrival, each story has a different starting point. That raises a fundamental question regarding organization. In what order does one tell the "story?" Opening with a statement that includes the reporter's name, date, time the call was received, the location, and the crime reported is a good way to start. It sets the stage and allows the writer to create a clear organizational structure. Next, the writer will want to introduce all the pertinent people and locations. From there, the writer can then describe the actions that took place, in the order that they happened. Should an individual arrive midway into the action or sequence of events, their arrival is simply part of the order of events. At the end of the report, the writer will have an opportunity to include any other important information including evidence such as photos or property and statements from the victim, witnesses, and, perhaps, the suspect. Any other relevant facts can be added in at that time as well. In this way, writers can ensure they provide organized and clear reports.

15. What is one of the most important elements of writing good reports?
    a. Details
    b. Organization
    c. Concise
    d. Providing the victim's timeline

16. Based on the passage, what is one of the biggest challenges of organizing a report?
    a. Remembering to include all the evidence
    b. Remembering what each witness said
    c. Determining what facts are relevant
    d. Determining the timeline to use

17. The best time to include evidence in the report is:
    a. At the end with other relevant information
    b. When it might appear in the timeline
    c. At the start, it's best to lay out all the facts
    d. Evidence should be submitted as a separate report

The next three questions are based on the following passage:

There are plenty of aspects of a police career that can be scary. Any situation an officer enters into can change rapidly and, as a result, produce physiological responses that increase stress. However, one situation that causes stress even without the added uncertainty is testifying in a court case. Officers enter unknown situations daily, so why is it that testifying in a court case, when an officer knows what is expected, what will happen, and when it will be, still so anxiety-producing? In part, many officers might feel as if the entire case and a resulting conviction rest entirely on their shoulders. However, it's also possible that a fear of public speaking, which is quite common, creates issues as well. Further, it requires an officer to trust a prosecutor and to understand they have little control over questions from an opposing attorney or judge. When officers are typically used to being either in control or creating order, this can be stressful. However, there are steps one can take to mitigate the anxiety and fear. First, officers should review the facts of the case as well as applicable laws, policies, and procedures. Familiarity with this information will breed confidence. Few things reduce stress more than taking control of what you can control. Next, anxiety is sometimes created when we don't know what the other attorney knows. For example, if you are testifying, the attorney has likely gathered information on you, so it's best to let a prosecutor know if anything from your personnel file might turn up. Again, this comes down to controlling what you. Lastly, anticipate the questions you may be asked and practice answering yes, no, or I don't know. Attorneys may try to trip you up with multi-layered compound questions and you can ask for clarification. Control what you can and be prepared for what you can't so you can alleviate a lot of the stress associate with testifying.

18. Based on the above passage, which of these contributes to the stress of testifying?
    a. Lack of control
    b. Lack of information
    c. Lack of experience
    d. Lack of support

19. According to the passage, what is one step an officer can take to ease the anxiety associated with testifying?
    a. Research the attorneys and judge
    b. Sit in on trials
    c. Practice public speaking
    d. Review the facts of the case

91

20. According to the passage, what should officers tell prosecutors?
   a. The facts of the case
   b. What is in their personnel file
   c. What they learned about the attorney and judge
   d. Reveal that they have anxiety about testifying

Written Expression

Directions: In the following sentences, choose the correct spelling of the missing word.

1. A non-violent breach of a law to bring about social change is called civil _____.
   a. disobidiance
   b. disobedense
   c. disobedience
   d. disobediance

2. After graduating from the Police Academy, an officer will be assigned to a _____.
   a. pricinct
   b. precint
   c. precinct
   d. presinct

3. Becoming a police officer is a great _____ to serve the community.
   a. oppurtinity
   b. opportunity
   c. opportinity
   d. oppurtunity

4. I _____ spilled coffee on my desk.
   a. acidentally
   b. assidentilly
   c. accidentilly
   d. accidentally

5. Your excellent work shows how _____ you are to the job.
   a. comited
   b. comitted
   c. commited
   d. committed

6. The veteran had a distinguished _____ career.
   a. milletary
   b. military
   c. militery
   d. miletary

7. The suspicious _____ was an unmarked metal tube.
   a. silinder
   b. sylinder
   c. cilinder
   d. cylinder

8. The deliveryman was confused when he tried to _____ the strange drop-off instructions.
   a. intirpret
   b. interpret
   c. intirprat
   d. interprat

9. The candidate was an upstanding _____ who wanted the best for her city.
   a. citisen
   b. sitizen
   c. citizen
   d. citesan

10. Due to the fine print, the item was not _____ for a rebate.
    a. elligable
    b. eligable
    c. elligible
    d. eligible

11. After the movie, they all proceeded to a nearby fast food _____.
    a. restaurant
    b. resturant
    c. restraunt
    d. restraunt

12. After the first incident, the department was more prepared for any _____ problems.
    a. subsequant
    b. subcequant
    c. subsequint
    d. subsequent

Directions: Read each sentence carefully and select the answer that is closest in meaning to the underlined word.

13. The company treasurer was found guilty of underlined embezzling $50,000 from the company's bank account to pay for the remodeling of his home.
    a. Bedazzling
    b. Stealing
    c. Decorating
    d. Borrowing

93

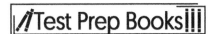

14. The judge <u>exonerated</u> Susan of all charges, so she left the courtroom a free woman.
    a. Cleared
    b. Executed
    c. Tried
    d. Convicted

15. When officers arrived on the scene of the deadly crash, they learned there had been one <u>fatality</u>.
    a. Birth
    b. Attraction
    c. Death
    d. Celebration

16. The unsuspecting art collector didn't realize the painting was a <u>forgery</u> until after it was appraised, so she became the 13th victim of the con artist.
    a. Antique
    b. Operation
    c. Sculpture
    d. Fake

17. The criminals wore gloves so they wouldn't leave behind any <u>latent</u> fingerprints.
    a. Hidden
    b. Painted
    c. Vinyl
    d. Visible

18. The state declared a <u>moratorium</u> on executions after new evidence cleared one death row inmate of his crime.
    a. Funeral
    b. Postponement
    c. Speech
    d. Hospitalization

19. The witness said the <u>perpetrator</u> wore a black ski mask and a blonde wig during the home invasion.
    a. Model
    b. Student
    c. Criminal
    d. Dancer

20. Though Miss Johnson swore to tell the truth under oath, she actually tried to <u>prevaricate</u> and claimed she didn't remember any details.
    a. Steal
    b. Impregnate
    c. Lie
    d. Confess

Memorization

Directions for the next five questions:

Examine the image below for two minutes then remove it from view. Answer the questions that follow the image without referring back to the image. Do not read the questions during the image review period.

1. How many people are in the room on the middle right?
    a. 1
    b. 2
    c. 3
    d. 4

2. How many cameras are there?
    a. 4
    b. 3
    c. 2
    d. 1

3. Which of the following items is in the room at the top?
    a. Stool
    b. Clock
    c. Camera
    d. Flag

4. What time is it on the clock?
    a. 11:15
    b. 1:55
    c. 10:30
    d. 2:35

5. How many officers are checking in at the bottom check-in station?
    a. 2
    b. 1
    c. 4
    d. 3

Directions for the next five questions:

Examine the image below for two minutes then remove it from view. Answer the questions that follow the image without referring back to the image. Do not read the questions during the image review period.

6. How many lanes of traffic are there?

    a. 3
    b. 6
    c. 4
    d. 2

7. How many miles are there until the exit 8?
    a. 1
    b. 3
    c. 4
    d. 6

8. What is hanging from the rearview mirror of the compact car?
    a. A basketball
    b. An air freshener
    c. A disco ball
    d. A soccer ball

9. Approximately how many cars are in the image?
    a. 10-15
    b. 15-20
    c. 20-30
    d. 30-40

10. How many airbags deployed in the accident?
    a. 1
    b. 2
    c. 3
    d. 4

Directions for the next five questions:

Examine the image below for two minutes then remove it from view. Answer the questions that follow the image without referring back to the image. Do not read the questions during the image review period.

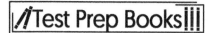

11. What is the hourly labor rate?
    a. $60/hr
    b. $40/hr
    c. $30/hr
    d. $50/hr

12. What letter is on one of the gunmen's baseball hat?
    a. V
    b. W
    c. S
    d. M

13. How many boxes are on the counter?
    a. 4
    b. 3
    c. 6
    d. 5

14. How many boxes are open?
    a. 4
    b. 1
    c. 2
    d. 3

15. How tall is the doorway?
    a. 6 feet
    b. 9 feet
    c. 8 feet
    d. 7 feet

Directions for the next five questions:

Examine the image below for two minutes then remove it from view. Answer the questions that follow the image without referring back to the image. Do not read the questions during the image review period.

101

16. According to the sign in the door, how many hours is the store open on Sunday?
   a. 12
   b. 8
   c. 11
   d. 10

17. What item is visible in the shopping bags?
   a. Eggs
   b. Toilet paper
   c. Steak
   d. Milk

18. What is written on the man's shirt?
   a. Sun
   b. Smile
   c. Surf
   d. Shore

19. What is the bicycle missing?
   a. Seat
   b. Tire
   c. Chain
   d. Lock

20. What item is the woman wearing?
   a. Pants
   b. Skirt
   c. Shorts
   d. A long coat

Inductive Reasoning

Use the following information to answer questions 1-2:

According to New York state law, members of a family or household are defined as two persons being in at least one of the following relationships:

(a) persons related by consanguinity or affinity;
(b) persons legally married to one another;
(c) persons formerly married to one another, regardless of whether they still reside in the same household;
(d) persons who have a child in common, regardless of whether such persons have been married or have lived together at any time; and
(e) persons who are not related by consanguinity or affinity and who are or have been in an intimate relationship, regardless of whether such persons have lived together at any time. Factors the court may consider in determining whether a relationship is an "intimate relationship" include but are not limited to: the nature or type of relationship, regardless of whether the relationship is sexual in nature; the frequency of interaction between the persons; and the duration of the relationship. Neither a casual acquaintance nor ordinary fraternization

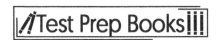

between two individuals in business or social contexts shall be deemed to constitute an "intimate relationship."

1. Based on the above criteria, what is the most significant element in determining if a relationship is considered "intimate" by New York law?
   a. The members' shared responsibility for one or more minors
   b. The members' emotional attachment to one another
   c. Whether or not the members have lived together
   d. The consanguinity of the members of the relationship

2. Which of the following statements reasonably explains the utility of this definition of a family or household?
   a. This passage defines family members during cases to determine child support.
   b. This passage defines households for the purposes of violations of tax write-offs.
   c. This passage's definition is useful for landlords determining the number of households that rent a residential building they own.
   d. This passage helps define close relationships to determine if a violation constitutes domestic violence.

3. A "contact" with a person experiencing homelessness is defined by the NYPD Patrol Guide as an interaction between an officer and such a person, with the result that the individual is transported to a shelter, is arrested or summoned, is treated as an emotionally disturbed person, or is requested to leave the location. What is a reasonable explanation for why a conversation without officer action is excluded from the "contact" types?
   a. The Patrol Guide's purpose is to tell officers how to act, not how to talk to members of the public.
   b. If the individual does not request assistance, then the officer does not need to report an interaction.
   c. If the interaction does not result in assistance or intervention by the officer, then it wasn't relevant to their duties.
   d. The definition expects the officer to have an actionable reason for contacting the individual.

Use the following information to answer questions 4-6.

> The following is part of the procedure for when an officer receives a noise complaint about a sound reproduction device. A sound reproduction device is any device with a speaker, amplifier, or other mechanism for producing sound (such as a radio).

I. Interview the complainant and alleged violator about the noise.
II. Determine if the noise is unreasonable.
III. Attempt to correct the condition by warning violator.
IV. If unable to correct the condition, issue a criminal summons.
    A. If a sound reproduction device is involved and the officer is able to lawfully access the device, seize the device as evidence.
    B. If the violator is under the age of eighteen, the device may not be seized.
    C. If the officer did not personally observe the violation, issue a civil summons.
V. If a sound reproduction device is seized, record the following in the summons:
    A. Circumstances that make the sound unreasonable

103

B. Number of complainants

C. Violator's refusal to comply

D. Distance from which the noise could be heard

E. Description of the device

VI. Prepare an invoice marked "evidence" and provide a copy to the violator as a receipt.

VII. If unable to correct the condition, determine if a warrantless entry is permissible based on exigent circumstances such as:

A. Dangerous overcrowding

B. Minors who appear intoxicated

C. Intoxicated persons who appear in need of medical attention

D. Presence or reliable information of violence

E. Allegations of sexual assault

4. Which of the following is a reasonable inference about minors present when an officer is responding to a noise complaint?
   a. Minors present during a noise violation are often engaged in reckless behavior.
   b. Noise violations by minors present less danger than violations by adults.
   c. The minors are not usually responsible for the complaint.
   d. Noise violations are typically associated with heavy intoxication.

5. If an officer seizes a sound reproduction device, what information is the officer NOT obligated to provide to the violator?
   a. The date of their court summons
   b. The distance from which the device could be heard
   c. The number and age of the complainants
   d. The exigent circumstances permitting the officer entry

6. Which of the following is a reasonable principle describing when an officer can enter a private residence hosting a party without a warrant?
   a. A warrant isn't needed to seize a sound reproduction device, although the officer can't continue to search the residence.
   b. The officer does not require a warrant if they can see harm being done to someone inside.
   c. Allegations of criminal behavior are never sufficient to justify warrantless entry.
   d. Warrantless entry to a residence is only permissible if the residents are not complying with the officer's directions.

7. If a lost child has been brought to the police and is being watched at the stationhouse, and then they are moved to another location, the Patrol Guide directs the officer to notify the Missing Persons squad. Which of the following is a reasonable explanation of this step in the procedure?
   a. Missing Persons can then begin to match the child against their database.
   b. Notifying Missing Persons helps avoid the moved child being marked erroneously as "missing."
   c. The Missing Persons squad can then begin to search for the child's guardians.
   d. If the child is no longer held at the stationhouse, then they are officially considered "missing."

8. The Patrol Guide states that "Information concerning a prisoner's or a victim's affliction with a communicable disease must be kept confidential. This information generally should not be released to the public, the media, the person's family and friends or to other prisoners." Which of the following statements is a reasonable inference from this guidance?
   a. Confidentiality of an individual's medical information is always required.
   b. Convicts have different rights concerning medical assistance than members of the public do.
   c. The purpose of this guidance is to avoid public panic over spreading communicable diseases.
   d. The purpose of this guidance is to restrict media access to sensitive information.

9. Officer Skylor is reading reports about crimes that occur in his patrol area.

> All drug deals reported occur between 19th Avenue and 45th Avenue, all house break-ins occur in the neighborhoods between Roosevelt and Van Buren, and all vehicle break-ins occur by the strip mall along Lakeshore School Road.

> Most drug deals happen on Fridays, most house break-ins occur on Mondays, and most vehicle break-ins occur on Wednesdays.

> Most drug deals happen between 8:00 p.m. and midnight, most house break-ins occur between 10:00 a.m. and 2:00 p.m., and most vehicle break-ins occur between 5:00 p.m. and 9:00 p.m.

Officer Skylor will have the best chance of decreasing vehicle break-ins if he patrols which of the following?
   a. The strip mall along Lakeshore School Road on Wednesdays from 4:00 p.m. to 10:00 p.m.
   b. The strip mall along Lakeshore School Road on Fridays from 7:00 p.m. to 1:00 a.m.
   c. The neighborhoods between Roosevelt and Van Buren on Monday from 9:00 a.m. to 3:00 p.m.
   d. Between 19th Avenue and 45th Avenue from 4:00 p.m. to 10:00 p.m.

10. Officer Tiffany is reading the crime reports in her patrol area.

> All drug deals reported occur between 19th Avenue and 45th Avenue, all house break-ins occur in the neighborhoods between Roosevelt and Van Buren, and all vehicle break-ins occur by the strip mall along Lakeshore School Road.

> Most drug deals happen on Fridays, most house break-ins occur on Mondays, and most vehicle break-ins occur on Wednesdays.

> Most drug deals happen between 8:00 p.m. and midnight, most house break-ins occur between 10:00 a.m. and 2:00 p.m., and most vehicle break-ins occur between 5:00 p.m. and 9:00 p.m.

Officer Tiffany will have the best chance of decreasing house break-ins if she patrols which of the following?
   a. The neighborhoods between Roosevelt and Van Buren on Monday from 4:00 p.m. to 10:00 p.m.
   b. The strip mall along Lakeshore School Road on Fridays from 7:00 p.m. to 1:00 a.m.
   c. The neighborhoods between Roosevelt and Van Buren on Monday from 9:00 a.m. to 3:00 p.m.
   d. Between 19th Avenue and 45th Avenue from 9:00 a.m. to 3:00 p.m.

Deductive Reasoning

1. For a crime to constitute a family offense, one of the criteria is that the crime harms an individual related by blood (consanguineous) who lives in the same household. Using this information, which of the following offenses is a family offense by merit of consanguinity?
   a. A forty-five-year-old man strikes his seven-year-old stepdaughter while at Central Park.
   b. A seventeen-year-old girl burns her thirteen-year-old brother with a cigarette while they're loitering outside a movie theater.
   c. A thirty-two-year-old woman threatens her thirty-five-year-old brother with a knife while he's visiting her home.
   d. A twenty-two-year-old man steals $159.00 from his great-grandfather's wallet while at a nursing facility.

Use the following information to answer questions 2-4:

> The court cases of persons aged sixteen or seventeen who are accused of committing a felony are handled by either the Family Court, or the Youth Part of the Supreme or County Court. The process by which court is chosen depends on if the felony was non-violent or violent. When tried in the Youth Part, the juvenile is treated as an adult, but their age is considered during sentencing.
>
> Non-violent felonies begin in the Youth Part and are transferred to the Family Court after thirty days. If the District Attorney (DA) wants to try the accused in the Youth Part, then the DA must file a motion describing the case's extraordinary circumstances.
>
> Violent felonies begin in the Youth Part and are transferred to the Family Court if they pass the 3-Part test. If the accusation involved significant physical injury, display of a weapon, or a sexual crime, the test is failed, and the felony is tried in the Youth Part.

2. Which of the following cases is tried in the Youth Part?
   a. On September 23, the DA initiates a case in which a sixteen-year-old boy is accused of felony assault on a seventeen-year-old boy, causing a concussion. They do not file a motion for extraordinary circumstances.
   b. On June 5, the DA initiates a case in which a fifteen-year-old girl is accused of shoplifting $1,200.00 of electronics. They file a motion for extraordinary circumstances on June 22.
   c. On February 9, the DA initiates a case in which a seventeen-year old girl is accused of felony stalking of a thirteen-year-old boy. They file a motion for extraordinary circumstances on March 12.
   d. On April 3, the DA initiates a case in which a seventeen-year-old boy is accused of misdemeanor menacing his mother with a kitchen knife. They do not file a motion for extraordinary circumstances.

3. Which of the following crimes passes the 3-Part test?
   a. Breaking someone's arm during a fight
   b. Recklessly driving through a red light
   c. Forcing a fellow student to perform oral sex
   d. Verbally harassing a teacher with repeated threats

4. A sixteen-year-old boy is accused of felony possession of fentanyl with the intent to sell the drug to other adolescents. In which court will he most likely be tried, and will he most likely be sentenced as a juvenile or as an adult?
   a. Youth Part, juvenile
   b. Youth Part, adult
   c. Family Court, juvenile
   d. Family Court, adult

5. A nightclub reports that its cash register was robbed. Camera surveillance reveals that a short individual with a brown hat and a black jacket stepped behind the bar and accessed the register. Recordings also show that the individual's ID was checked on the way into the club, and that they left the same way. Which of the following suspects is the most likely culprit?
   a. John, a 5' 7" tall man with brown hair and blue eyes who is twenty-two years old
   b. Alice, a 5' 2" tall woman found wearing a brown baseball cap and black jacket who is nineteen years old
   c. Robert, a 5' 1" tall man who works for the nightclub who is twenty-nine years old
   d. Fatima, a 5' 0" tall woman with black hair and brown eyes who is twenty-four years old

Use the following information to answer questions 6-7:

> An NYPD officer may use deadly force when the officer reasonably believes that it is necessary to protect themselves or another person from an imminent threat of serious injury or death.
>
> Deadly force is considered any use of force—such as discharging one's firearm—that is capable of causing death or serious physical injury.
>
> The reasonableness of using force is considered from the perspective of the officer at the time force was used. Information outside what the officer could have known is not considered when determining the reasonableness of deadly force. Some other factors considered when reviewing if deadly force was reasonable include the following:
>
> - The crime's severity
> - The immediacy of the threat presented by the suspect
> - The potential for collateral injury to other persons
> - Personal characteristics of the officer and/or the suspect
> - Environmental circumstances

6. Which of the following situations most likely constitutes a reasonable use of deadly force?
   a. Striking an assailant's wrist to dislodge their hand from a civilian's neck
   b. Striking a suspect's throat after they've grasped the officer's firearm
   c. Using a firearm from fifteen yards away as a suspect uses a knife to stab a civilian in a crowd of about twenty-five people
   d. Using a firearm to stop a short, gray-haired woman running at the officer

7. An officer shares the following account during a review of their use of deadly force: "I radioed dispatch after the car pulled over, and when I got out of my vehicle, I didn't realize that the young man had done the same. I directed him twice to return to his vehicle, and he did not answer. I directed him to put his hands on the roof of his vehicle, and the man did so. I walked over to tell him this was just a traffic stop—the car had been going about ten over—but he didn't move, so I stepped closer. He smelled drunk but hadn't been driving badly. Once I was next to him the man turned and hit me in the chin. I fell down, and he climbed on top of me. I felt his hands on my chest when I reached for my firearm, and I fired upward. He went limp and I pushed him off, then radioed dispatch for an ambulance." Why was this use of deadly force reasonable?
   a. The suspect was not complying with the officer's repeated requests.
   b. The suspect was a threat to others because he was driving while intoxicated.
   c. There was imminent danger to the officer of being choked by the suspect.
   d. The suspect was significantly stronger than the officer, and use of less force was unlikely to reduce the danger.

8. A woman is pulled over for swerving between lanes. Her papers are in order, but her speech is slurred, and she appears visibly very nervous. She was also driving 50 mph in a zone with a limit of 45 mph. Which of the following statutes would define this crime?
   a. The statute that prohibits driving while intoxicated
   b. The statute that requires all vehicles to be insured
   c. The statute that prohibits going over the designated speed limit
   d. The statute that prohibits suicide

9. Federal law has a statute that prohibits minors under twenty-one years of age from purchasing alcohol. Which of the following crimes can be defined using this statute?
   a. A man with gray hair and a long beard is found stealing beer from a convenience store.
   b. Gun shots were reportedly heard at a public park.
   c. There are reports of music being played too loud from an apartment late at night.
   d. A nightclub bouncer is reported to not be checking IDs before letting people enter the bar area.

10. OFFICER'S REPORT: I responded to a call about a missing eight-year-old child in Tempe, AZ, around midnight. When I arrived, a woman, calling herself Joan Fountain, identified herself as the mother of the lost child, James Fountain. She said the child usually never leaves the apartment complex, only going from his apartment to where his friend lives, but he has not been there and has not come back since the morning he was supposed to have left for school. He also will not answer his cell phone. She also says the school called and informed her he was absent from school that day. She seemed intoxicated and got irritated easily at my questions. Also, the child's bike was missing, and change was taken from a tray where the family kept loose coins.

Which of the following details in the report is NOT relevant to the case?
   a. The woman being intoxicated
   b. The missing bike and money
   c. The time of night
   d. The name of the mother

11. A man is discovered dead in his house, surrounded by drug paraphernalia and a half-empty bottle of liquor. Which of the following details in a case report would be the most relevant to the situation?
a. The square footage of the house
b. The type of shoes the man was wearing
c. The type of drug paraphernalia found
d. The number of officers present at the scene on arrival

12. An officer would MOST likely require backup in which of the following situations?
a. There is a report of gang violence in a neighborhood.
b. A young man is caught shoplifting from the grocery store.
c. A man is accused of sexual assault at his workplace.
d. A woman reports a missing purse containing very expensive jewelry.

13. An officer is MOST likely to ask an individual to step out of their car for inspection after pulling them over for which of the following?
a. The driver has outdated insurance.
b. There are five teenagers in the car with no adults present.
c. The driver was speeding.
d. There is a strong odor of alcohol on the driver's breath.

Use the following witness reports for questions 14-15:

WITNESS REPORT 1: An elderly man I have never seen before came into the office just before noon and asked to speak privately with the boss and then, without waiting, just barged through the boss's door. About ten minutes later, I heard two gunshots, one right after the other, I think, or maybe a few minutes apart. When I went back into the office, both men were lying dead, and the gun was on the floor between them. Before the man entered the office, I asked my boss if he could come in first, of course, and he said sure. I didn't see him go in, though, but I was pretty busy, so I don't know.

WITNESS REPORT 2: Raul, a middle-aged man who worked with us at the factory and who I spoke with in the mornings occasionally before work, told me that day he was going to see the boss about wages. He didn't sound upset, but you never know with Raul. He was a mysterious fellow. I don't know when he went to the office because I didn't see him go, but I remember hearing the shots around noon because I was just about to go to lunch.

WITNESS REPORT 3: We were all about to go to lunch at noon when Raul, my partner on the factory line who comes to lunch with us every day, says he is skipping the day because he needs to speak with the boss. He had been there awhile, but he was only forty or so, not like us old timers who got on because of a whole government layoff thing. Sure, we were kind of upset about stuff here and there, but I don't think I heard him say anything really. He wouldn't talk to anyone but me about it too because it wasn't that serious and he was a private man. I mean I liked my boss. Sometimes he was mean or didn't treat us right, but he was just a man, I guess. I don't really talk about the company. I just do my work, and I don't talk to Raul really either.

WITNESS REPORT 4: I didn't really see it happen, but I knew it would. I never trust anyone in this company. They all just got hired because of some dirty government business. I didn't know or speak to Raul, or any of them, except I guess one morning we all kind of had a discussion, but I wasn't really involved, I swear! Don't question me anymore!

Test Prep Books

14. Which of the following details is most likely true?
    a. The shooting happened around noon.
    b. There was no discussion among workers that day.
    c. Raul is a very old man.
    d. Raul is shy.

15. Which witness is most likely telling the truth?
    a. Witness 1
    b. Witness 2
    c. Witness 3
    d. Witness 4

Information Ordering and Problem Sensitivity

1. While an officer is away from the stationhouse, they turn the key in their vehicle's ignition twice, and the vehicle does not start. Which of the following steps is most likely to come first while responding to this situation?
    a. Describing the vehicle's recent functioning to a mechanic
    b. Contacting dispatch to report the vehicle's malfunction
    c. Checking that the officer is using the correct key
    d. Calling the police department's preferred towing service

2. While on subway patrol, Officer Wilcox was flagged down by a younger man, who identified himself as Robert May. Mr. May wished to report that his over-the-shoulder computer bag had been stolen while travelling on the subway. According to Mr. May, he had been exiting the train at a busy station he was unfamiliar with, and had stopped once on the platform to orient himself. There were two staircases on either side of where he was, each one leading to a transfer for a different line. Mr. May reported looking to his right first, and upon seeing that that set of stairs led to the wrong transfer, turned his head to look at the other staircase. Upon turning, he was bumped into by a man walking directly at him, causing the both of them to drop the items they were holding. In the midst of all that was going on, Mr. May lost track of his computer bag, which itself had not fallen but which he had placed down. It was not until all the other items had been recovered that Mr. May noticed the bag missing. He then reported that he turned around and saw a man who had been walking alongside the individual who had bumped into him walking over in the same direction and up the stairs. Mr. May attempted to pursue the individual, but found it difficult to keep up and keep track of where the individual went. He presumed the individual left the station, but upon doing so himself he realized he could not see the individual. He then returned to the station and flagged down Officer Wilcox.

Which way did the individual Mr. May claimed stole his computer bag go after grabbing it, according to Mr. May?
    a. He went onto the train Mr. May had just exited.
    b. He remained in the area, blending into the crowd, until Mr. May left the area himself.
    c. He left in the same direction the man Mr. May bumped into was headed, up the staircase Mr. May first turned to upon exiting the train.
    d. He doubled back, heading up the staircase Mr. May originally intended to go up.

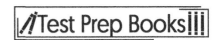

3. Officer Mullen responded to an incident involving a physical altercation outside of a liquor store. Present at the scene were the three individuals involved in the altercation, as well as the store owner and the cashier. According to the cashier, the three individuals often came in together, and would frequently pool their money together and share their purchase. The cashier explained that once the individuals were outside of the store, she began to hear loud bickering regarding how much each individual was drinking. She then reported hearing expletives before the sound of glass shattering. Two of the individuals involved in the altercation, a man and a woman, initially refused to cooperate with Officer Mullen. The third individual, however, the individual who had seemingly borne the brunt of the aggressions, was willing to speak to the Officer. They told the Officer that the other two were "bad friends" of theirs who had resorted to get their money however they could. The individual, who refused to identify themselves, said that the woman present had brought a half full bottle of liquor down on top of their head, causing a number of smaller wounds as well as fairly substantial gash above their right eye. After receiving that statement, Officer Mullen returned to speak with the couple, who now were more willing to cooperate after seeing the other individual involved come forward. The man spoke first, claiming that it was an accident, and the bottle had slipped during a bad joke, before the woman spoke over him and informed the Officer that that other individual present was lying, and that in fact she was always trying to leach money from them.

What claim did the first individual involved in the altercation that Officer Mullen spoke to make?
   a. They claimed that it was an accident, the result of a joke gone bad.
   b. They claimed the other two individuals were always trying to take their money and that the woman present attacked them.
   c. They claimed the woman present was jealous of their relationship with the men present, and had attacked them as a result.
   d. They claimed the man present was jealous of their relationship with the woman present, and had attacked them as a result.

Use the following passage to answer questions 4-6:

When a principal inquires if a student in their care qualifies for a "safety transfer" per the No Child Left Behind Act, it is the Neighborhood Coordination Sergeant's duty to complete a records search to determine if a qualifying incident has occurred, and then report that to the principal. A qualifying incident is a violent crime which takes place on public school grounds at the school the victim attends. The sergeant performs this task using the following procedure.

   I. Confirm the request was initiated by the principal.
   II. Confirm that the request includes:
      A. The school's name;
      B. The date, time, and location of the alleged incident;
      C. And the name of the victim;
      D. Otherwise, the request is invalid.
   III. Consult records of complaints submitted by the victim on the specified date.
   IV. Records systems shall be consulted in the following order until the report is found:
      A. OMNIFORM System
      B. Online Juvenile Report System
      C. School Safety Division Criminal Incident Reports
      D. Aided Report

111

       E. Precinct Detective Squad

       F. School Safety Division Operations Center

  V. If reports are unclear about whether the incident was classified as unfounded, question the assigned detective.

  VI. Prepare a report for the principal no later than the next school day after the request was made. This shall include:

       A. Whether a report was filed;

       B. Whether the incident is alleged to have occurred at the public school;

       C. Whether the alleged crime is a qualifying incident;

       D. And whether the incident was classified as unfounded.

  VII.   Record the following:

       A. The time the request was answered

       B. The person receiving the report

       C. Whether or not the alleged crime was a qualifying incident

       D. Whether or not the incident was classified as unfounded

4. Which of the following is the principal expected to do first?
   a. Consult the OMNIFORM system.
   b. Answer whether a report was filed.
   c. Record the time the request was answered.
   d. Submit a request to the police department.

5. If the Online Juvenile Report System indicates that the alleged crime does not constitute a qualifying incident, what should the sergeant do next?
   a. Prepare the report to provide an answer to the principal.
   b. Consult the School Safety Division Criminal Incident Reports.
   c. Question the detective to determine if the incident was unfounded.
   d. Question the victim to determine if the alleged crime was a qualifying incident.

6. When should the sergeant contact a detective for further information?
   a. Before recording the time of their answer to the principal
   b. After consulting the OMNIFORM system
   c. After confirming that the request has all requisite information
   d. When determining if the allegations are well founded

Use the following passage to answer questions 7 and 8:

> NYPD officers are required to complete the following fingerprint procedure after all arrests, except in the case of hospitalized prisoners.

  I. Record the check digit from the On Line Booking System.

  II. Use the LIVESCAN machine to fingerprint and palmprint the prisoner as follows:

       A. Ensure that the prisoner's hands are clean and dry.

         II.A.i.   If the prisoner's hands are excessively dry, use a Pre-Scan Pad.

       B. Ensure that the LIVESCAN scanner is clean and dry.

       C. Enter the check digit into the LIVESCAN.

D. Fingerprint flat impressions of the four fingers on the large platen and the thumbs on the small platen.

E. Press SAVE after the impression is completed, and the hand is removed from the platen.

F. Fingerprint individual fingers on the small platen.

    II.F.i.   Follow the LIVESCAN machine's prompts for finger order.

    II.F.ii.   Center the core of each finger on the cross lines.

    II.F.iii.   Roll each individual finger to one side as directed by the arrow.

    II.F.iv.   Press SCAN.

    II.F.v.   After the roll is complete, press SAVE if the image is acceptable.

G. Palmprint palms on large platen and press SCAN.

III. If a print cannot be taken, then annotate that print's box with an explanation.

IV. After fingerprinting the prisoner, check LIVESCAN transmit queue to confirm that prints are being sent.

7. How should an officer begin to record the right index fingerprint of a prisoner?
   a. Roll the right index finger across the large platen.
   b. Center the right index finger on the small platen.
   c. Press the four fingers onto the large platen.
   d. Enter the check digit into the LIVESCAN machine.

8. When is a damp pad used during the fingerprinting process?
   a. To clean the large platen after recording the four fingers
   b. To clean the small platen between individual fingers
   c. To clean the prisoner's hands prior to fingerprinting
   d. To moisten the prisoner's hands if they are too dry

9. At 3:34 AM on Wednesday, January 6th, Officer Gonzales received a call from dispatch regarding a reported breaking-and-entering at an apartment building. Officer Gonzales arrived at the scene and spoke with Evelyn Townsend, the individual who made the call. She explained to the Officer that the individual who had broken into her apartment was an estranged friend of hers, and that the friend was still in the apartment. The Officer then asked Ms. Townsend to recount the events leading to her calling. She explained that, upon returning home from a party, she noticed several large trash bags in the hallway outside her door, and upon closer inspection she found that the bags were full of much of her stuff. Ms. Townsend then attempted to enter the apartment, only to find that the chain latch was on the door. It was at this point that Ms. Townsend began to suspect her estranged friend was the individual inside her apartment, and she yelled out her name in order to identify herself. Although she did not see her friend, Ms. Townsend reports hearing her friend's voice yell out in response. Furthermore, she said this kind of behavior would not be atypical of her friend, and that her friend most likely gained access to the apartment through a window in the bathroom, which is typically left open and is accessible via the back of the apartment building. Officer Gonzales then approached the apartment building and knocked, although at this point loud music had begun to play from somewhere in the apartment. After using a key provided by Ms. Townsend to open the door to the apartment, Officer Townsend identified himself through the open door, after which time the music stopped and shuffling could be heard. A few minutes later the estranged friend opened the door to the apartment, apologizing to the Officer and asking if she could go home. Ms. Townsend declined to press charges, and the friend was soon released.

According to Ms. Townsend, what is the most likely way her estranged friend gained access to her property?
  a. She entered through the front door using a key provided by Ms. Townsend.
  b. She entered through the front door by slipping through the crack in the front door, which was chained shut.
  c. She entered through the window in the bathroom, which is typically left open.
  d. She entered through the windows in the bathroom, which she broke open with a hammer.

10. A concerned citizen made an anonymous 911 call regarding a case of suspected parental abuse in his apartment building. According to the caller, the family living across from them would often have loud screaming matches with their children, whom the caller estimated as being about 12 and 9. Multiple times the caller had heard the children scream out in what he believed to be pain, followed by a loud male voice instructing them to be quiet. The caller also informed the police that the he believed, but had not heard, that the mother and grandmother present also physically disciplined the children. There was an older male figure present in the apartment, whom the caller had seen but had never heard. The caller told the 911 operator that he had been prompted to call when he saw one of the children leaving for school with a black eye.

According to the caller, how many individuals has he witnessed residing in the apartment?
  a. 4
  b. 3
  c. 6
  d. 5

11. Officer Jefferson responded to a report of a robbery at a local bodega. Upon arriving at the scene, Officer Jefferson spoke to the individual manning the register of the store, who identified himself as Tito. Tito informed the Officer that a number of individuals, who Tito has seen before and believes to be students at a local high school, ran into the store at a quarter past four and began grabbing as many items as they could off of the shelves. When Tito and others present attempted to stop the individuals, there were a series of physical altercations, including one officer of a local fire station who was slammed against the freezer by multiple individuals after attempting to grab the stolen items away. All the individuals wore identical ski masks during the encounter, which Officer Jefferson could see verified on the camera footage of the incident. Tito claimed to the Officer that he could easily identify the individuals if needed.

Who did Tito, the cashier at the bodega, believe was responsible for the robbery?
  a. Students of a local high school.
  b. Officers at a local fire station.
  c. He does not know, and claims he would not be able to identify them if needed.
  d. He does not know, but claims he could identify them if needed.

12. Officers began receiving numerous reports about suspicious activity at an empty lot, and Officers Lewis and Powell were dispatched to the location as a result. The officers arrived at the empty lot at around 1:30pm, and found no individuals present. However, there was evidence of illicit drug use, specifically hypodermic needles and marijuana joint filters, which supported the common theory that the area was used by drug dealers. However, since no one was present at the site at the time, the Officers simply reported what they observed and continued their normal patrol. That night, at approximately 2:30am, Officers Martin and Machado were again dispatched to the site, after receiving multiple reports in a relatively short span of time. One report specifically had claimed that armed individuals were present at the site, so the Officers proceeded with caution. Upon arriving at the scene, they reported seeing a small group of individuals who seemed to be trying to keep a low profile. After establishing contact with the group, the Officers discovered a number of drug users using the spot, however there was no evidence that any selling of drugs was occurring. However, the individuals were trespassing on the lot, which was privately owned. When this was explained, and the individuals were made aware of the number of reports that had been made about their activity, the individuals agreed to leave.

What did the first officers to inspect the empty lot find?
   a. They found several armed, unidentified individuals, and promptly called for back-up.
   b. They found a group of drug users, who were trespassing on the privately owned lot but otherwise committing no crimes.
   c. They found an individual selling illicit drugs, and a number of individuals purchasing from him.
   d. They found no one, but did discover evidence of illicit drug use at the site.

13. Officer Beasley responded to a call from dispatch concerning a report of a physical altercation between two individuals believed to be intoxicated. Upon arriving at the scene, the Officer spoke to the two gentlemen involved in the incident, who identified themselves as Oliver Foley and Alec Gardner as well as an independent bystander who witnessed the altercation and the lead up to it. The Officer spoke with the independent bystander first, who reported that she witnessed Mr. Foley and Mr. Gardner yelling at each other for several minutes in a public park, with Mr. Foley standing off to the side of a footpath and Mr. Gardner sitting on a nearby park bench. She attested that the physical altercation began when Mr. Gardner stood up off the bench and approached Mr. Foley, who then reacted by pushing Mr. Gardner hard down against the bench. Mr. Foley, who the Officer spoke with first, claimed the altercation began when he approached Mr. Gardner and asked if he could take a seat next to him on the bench. Mr. Foley then alleged that Mr. Gardner began to hurl insults and expletives at him, including several that insinuated Mr. Foley was a prostitute. At some point in this tirade, Mr. Foley claimed, Mr. Gardner stood up and bumped into him, which prompted Mr. Foley to react by pushing off against him. Mr. Gardner, when speaking to the Officer, claimed that Mr. Foley had approached him attempting to solicit money in exchange for sex, to which Mr. Gardner had immediately refused and stood up off the bench, prompting Mr. Foley to push him back down.

According to the independent bystander, how long were Mr. Foley and Mr. Gardner engaged in a verbal altercation because the physical altercation occurred?
- a. For several hours; she had come through the park multiple times and witnessed their argument before it turned physical.
- b. For a few minutes; after a bit, Mr. Gardner stood up off the bench and the physical altercation began.
- c. For only a few seconds; shortly after Mr. Foley first walked up to Mr. Gardner, Mr. Gardner stood up and the altercation began.
- d. Mr. Foley and Mr. Gardner did not engage in a verbal altercation, according to the bystander; their fight began almost immediately once they encountered each other.

14. Officer Orozco was dispatched to a construction site due to reports of missing and potentially stolen equipment. Once on site, she spoke with Kelly Phillips, the foreman present on the site. According to Mr. Phillips, a number of items and pieces of important equipment had been going missing from the site since before official construction even began. Several pieces of surveying equipment had been stolen when the site was first inspected, with much of the rest of the equipment being vandalized and destroyed. According to Mr. Phillips, there was a fair degree of unhappiness in the local community regarding the new project, which had replaced a beloved local institution that couldn't afford to keep up on rent. Harassment of the workers themselves had occurred at first, but Mr. Phillips said that most community individuals seemed to eventually understand that the workers themselves were not responsible. It was then that the site saw an uptick in items going missing, Mr. Phillips told Officer Orozco. Extra tarps, protective equipment, building materials – every week there seemed to be some new missing. For the most part, the company responsible for the project was happy to simply foot the bill and replace the missing items, so the suspected thefts had gone unreported, but Mr. Phillips took it upon himself to inform the police when he found large construction equipment and tools missing, including several jackhammers.

According to Mr. Phillips, what were the first items to go missing from the construction site?
- a. Valuables belonging to construction workers, as initially community resentment was aimed at those individuals.
- b. Building materials and extra tarps.
- c. Large construction tools, including jackhammers.
- d. Surveying equipment, which was stolen before actual construction on the project had begun.

15. Officer Anderson was dispatched to an apartment building, where a resident reported having witnessed some form of home invasion occur. When the Officer arrived at the apartment building, the caller, who identified herself as Edith Terrell, pointed out which unit she had seen the home invasion occur in, and proceeded to recount to the Officer exactly what she had seen occur. Ms. Terrell reported that shortly after arriving home to her own apartment, she noticed that the door to the ground floor apartment across the street was propped open, and all the lights were on. Although Ms. Terrell did not personally know the family living in the unit, she knew the approximate ages and relationships of all members of the family, and testified that she hadn't noticed any of them about the apartment in a number of days. Due to the age of the family's children and time of year, Ms. Terrell hypothesized that the family may have been somewhere on summer vacation. Although she at first assumed maybe the family had just arrived home, and that's why the door had been propped over, Ms. Terrell then described to Officer Anderson watching four men, all wearing full face respirator masks, flee the apartment with several duffel bags full of items.

116

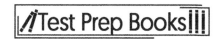

According to Ms. Terrell, what was the first irregularity she noticed that alerted her to the ongoing home invasion?

    a.   She noticed that the door to the apartment was propped open and all the lights were on.

    b.   She noticed the family had not returned from their family vacation when they told her.

    c.   She noticed the children of the family sitting outside the apartment without their parents around.

    d.   She noticed four men, all wearing full face respirator masks, fleeing the apartment with duffel bags.

16. Officer Fisher was dispatched to an artisanal coffee shop due to a report that a disgruntled customer was refusing to leave despite being asked to do so. When Officer Fisher arrived, she discovered that the situation had escalated; a full-on screaming match was occurring between the manager of the shop and the customer over the counter, while the rest of the employees huddled over in the far corner. What few customers remained were either trying to help the manager de-escalate or record the incident. After escorting the customer out of the shop, Officer Fisher spoke to the customer, the manager, and a number of witnesses. The manager claimed that the customer had a personal vendetta against one particular barista working there, and came to the coffee shop to confront them. When the barista made it clear they did not want to speak with them further, the manager asked the customer to leave, at which the customer sat on the floor and refused to move. Although initially allowing the customer to say there, the customer began harassing others in the store, telling them not to tip their barista. After asking the customer once more to leave, the manager made the decision to call the police. When the customer was informed the police were on their way, she reportedly began to get aggressive, culminating in her grabbing the barista over the counter and pouring hot coffee on her. The barista, who informed the Officer that the customer had done similar things at previous jobs she had had, but that she did not to press charges, was fortunately uninjured, though shaken up.

According to the manager, what is the first thing the disgruntled customer did when asked to leave the coffee shop?

    a.   She spilled out the tip jar all over the floor of the store.

    b.   She assaulted the barista, pouring hot coffee on her.

    c.   She sat on the floor of the stop, refusing to move.

    d.   She left, waiting outside for the barista to get off of work.

17. Officer Delacruz was dispatched to a small regional airport, where pilots and other employees were reporting being flashed with lasers as they came onto the runway. The employee who called 911 claimed he had witnessed teenagers sneak in through a hole in the fencing around the runway that led out to a wooded area, and claimed that the airport had experienced similar problems in the past. When Officer Delacruz arrived at the area in question, they found no one there, but did find evidence of recent activity in the area, including multiple cigarette butts, beer cans and marks left by the stakes of camping chairs. Officer Delacruz returned the next day, following more reports of lasers being flashed. This time, they spotted a couple of men dressed in heavy camouflage crouching in the wooded area. Upon making their presence known, the men came out. They told Officer Delacruz they had been hunting in the area the day prior and had stumbled across the area, although the men did not have rifles on them that day. When asked why they thought it was a good idea to flash lasers at planes, the men admitted they had been drinking on both occasions.

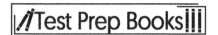

Who did the 911 caller claim was responsible for the flashing of lasers?
   a. Disgruntled airport workers looking to blow off steam.
   b. Hunters who had stumbled across the area through a hole in the fence.
   c. Teenagers who had snuck onto the runway through a hole in the fence.
   d. A pilot with a complex.

18. Officer Gutierrez was one of the first officers present at a hostage situation in a child care center. She was informed by another officer present at the scene that an estranged parent had entered the center with a knife and demanded that his child be allowed to leave with him. When the director of the center refused to release the child to the man, he apparently barred the front door. At that point, there were eight children present in the center, including the man's child, and four other adults, including the director. However, almost all of the children and all the adults save one were quickly able to exit the center through a back door. However, the director, the man's child, and another child in the front office who was there to use the first aid kit were still in the room with the man.

When Officer Gutierrez first arrived at the hostage situation, how many individuals were still inside the child care center?
   a. Thirteen; twelve hostages and the estranged parent.
   b. Two; just the estranged parent and their child.
   c. Three; the estranged parent, their children and the director.
   d. Four; the estranged parent, their children, the director and another child.

19. Officers Cohen and Johnson were on patrol at a subway station, when they were informed of a man acting aggressively on the incoming train. When the train arrived, the Officers stopped the train and located the individual, who at that point was one of only a few people in the final few cars of the train. The other passengers present later informed the Officers that the man had scared away most of the people sitting in the last few cars. One individual attested that the man had previously been passed out on the train for several stops, and had only become aggressive when he was jostled awake by the train. When the Officers attempted to communicate with the man, they found he was mostly incoherent, and clearly intoxicated. There was a broken glass bottle near the man full of what appeared to liquor, and eyewitnesses claimed he had been waving the glass bottle aggressively at other passengers. From what the Officers could understand from the man, it seems he felt as if someone on the train had jostled him awake, and everything else from there had been a misunderstanding between him and the others on the train.

According to the other individuals on the train, what was the man doing prior to threatening other train passengers?
   a. He was asleep, and had been for some time.
   b. He had been going around waking up other individuals sleeping on the subway.
   c. He had been arguing loudly with other passengers, but was not aggressive until he began drinking.
   d. He had come onto the train threatening people, so none of the eyewitnesses on the train could attest to what he had been doing before.

20. Officer Cunningham was called to a local high school due to a 911 call from a concerned citizen. The caller, who declined to identify herself but asserted she was a concerned citizen living near the school, claimed there were armed gang members in and around the school's property. When asked by the 911 operator to clarify what exactly she had seen, the caller explained that she had seen a group of young men smoking a joint on the blacktop outside of the school. When asked for specifics of how many men

118

there were and how many were armed, she claimed she couldn't remember exactly how many, and that she hadn't seen the weapons but she could tell the men were carrying firearms based on how they carried themselves. When Officer Cunningham arrived at the school, he saw no immediate evidence of any gang activity on the site, and proceeded to speak with an administrator at the school regarding the claim. The administrator leveled with the officer when asked about what the concerned citizen had reported, and admitted that there had been an ongoing problem at the school with students sneaking out of the building to smoke and skip class. However, the administrator asserted, there were metal detectors at all entrances to the school, so she highly doubted anyone was carrying a weapon on them. Upon examining the site, Officer Cunningham found a number of half-smoked joints, and spoke to a custodial worker taking his smoke break nearby, who claimed he knew the group of kids who smoked out by there and that they weren't a danger to anyone.

What was the initial claim made by the 911 caller?
- a. She claimed she had smelled marijuana smoke in the air, and suspected someone was smoking on school property.
- b. She claimed there were armed gang members in and around the school's property.
- c. She claimed she saw custodial workers smoking marijuana on the school's property.
- d. She claimed she saw several men wielding and aiming firearms in and around the school's property.

21. Officers Love and Hansen were dispatched to a nearby public park due to multiple reports of indecent exposure. Upon arriving to the park, the Officers were quickly able to assess the situation. The individual, a middle-aged woman, had stripped off all of her clothes and was frantically running about a large open green area. By the time the Officers had arrived, a large crowd of spectators had gathered, and some individuals were attempting to speak to the woman and calm her down. The Officers initially attempted to do the same, but upon seeing the Officers the woman only became more frantic, desperately shouting for them to get away from her. Seeing that she did not pose an immediate danger to herself or anyone else, the Officers backed away, which seemed to relieve the woman slightly. Speaking to some of the nearby witnesses, the Officers learned that the woman had been in this state for at least half an hour, and the general consensus seemed to be that she chose to remove her clothes in order to go swimming in the public fountain. Although most of the individuals had not seen the woman prior to this, one individual claimed they had seen the woman a few hours before on a nearby green space, and told the Officers they would be able to identify the blanket the woman had brought with her. Upon approaching the area, the eyewitness pointed to a vibrant orange blanket on which a man lay sleeping. The individual on the blanket, who initially was disoriented when awoken by the Officers, then admitted to them that both he and the woman had taken hallucinogenic drugs when they got to the park, and that he had not seen her since the two of them got in a verbal confrontation and she stormed off. Understanding the situation, the Officers were able to take appropriate steps to properly de-escalate the situation with the woman, who felt incredibly embarrassed when she eventually calmed down and came to.

According to the eyewitnesses in the park, why had the woman originally taken off her clothes?
- a. No one was really sure – by the time anyone noticed her, she was already naked.
- b. They claimed she had stripped off her clothes in response to a fight she was having with her boyfriend.
- c. They claimed she had taken her clothes off after taking hallucinogenic drugs.
- d. They claimed she had initially stripped naked in order to go swimming in the public fountain.

22. Officers Yang and Hawkins were on patrol near a subway station when they received notice that a group of young men had been shaking down people seeking to board the train. As they headed down to the station, they flagged down a station employee, who informed them the men were off to the left side of the station, and would most likely flee out the nearest exit if approached by police. Officer Yang then decided to exit the station and man the exit the men would mostly likely have to leave through. Once he was in position, Officer Hawkins went through into the station and approached the men, who quickly identified the Officer and began to flee. Due to where the men were located, it was impossible for Officer Hawkins to get an accurate count of how many individuals there were, but it appeared that at least some had fled in the direction of Officer Yang. The others, perhaps recognizing the trap, tried to evade Officer Hawkins themselves by simply all running past him. He was able to detain two of the individuals as they ran by him, but three more got by him and escaped out the entrance the Officers had originally come through. After detaining and handcuffing both men, Officer Hawkins regrouped with Officer Yang, who reported four individuals had left through the exit he was guarding, three of which he was able to detain.

Based on Officer Hawkins and Yang's observations, how many men were involved in the shake down, and how many of the men involved evaded capture?
   a. There were nine men involved, and four evaded capture.
   b. There were ten men involved, and five evaded capture.
   c. There were five men involved, and no one evaded capture.
   d. There were nine men involved, and no one evaded capture.

23. A young woman called the police, and said she thought her apartment neighbor might be a serial killer. As she explained to the operator, she had recently moved into the neighborhood, and had been feeling on edge after a spate of recent home invasions and assaults on women in the area. A few days prior, she had been working a night shift at her job, and upon returning home to her apartment was greeted in the lobby by the young man who lived in the apartment directly across from her. On top of the oddness of meeting someone out so late, she became suspicious and quickly terrified when she realized he had blood splatter all over his sleeves, which she could see peeking out under his parka. That night, she claimed she heard a woman screaming and the sound of heavy machinery coming from the man's apartment. She claimed she rarely had seen the man during the day, and generally found him to be pretty reclusive. Officer Hudson was dispatched to the man's apartment, who introduced himself as Igor Belyaev. Mr. Belyaev, who had recently immigrated from Europe, informed Officer Hudson that he had been working night shifts at his uncle's butchers' shop, and claimed he usually did not change his shirt after work, preferring to toss a parka over it and just worry about it when he got home. When Officer Hudson specifically asked about his activities the night prior, Mr. Belyaev claimed he had had trouble sleeping that night, and resorted to working on a personal carpentry project in order to tire himself out.

Which of the suspicious details reported by the 911 caller did Mr. Belyaev not provide an explanation for?
   a. Why he was up so late, and in general why she had not seen him much.
   b. Why she heard a woman screaming coming from his apartment late at night.
   c. Why he had blood stains on his shirt.
   d. Why she heard the sounds of heavy machinery coming from his apartment late at night.

120

24. The mother of a young woman entered the police station and filled a report with Officer Potts, claiming that her daughter's fiancé was stalking her. When asked to clarify, the woman, who identified herself solely as Rachel, said that she had long suspected her daughter's fiancé of wanting to seduce and sleep with her, and claimed that she had evidence that he was monitoring her phone and bank records, and showed the Officer explicit texts and pictures that appeared to be from the fiancé. Officer Potts told the woman she would investigate, and that she should feel safe knowing the police were looking into it. Shortly after Rachel left the station, Officer Potts received a frantic call from Rachel, in which she told the Officer the fiancé had been waiting for her at her house. Officer Potts, fearing for Rachel's safety, headed over to the address Rachel had provided her. Upon arriving, Officer Potts was greeted by the woman's daughter, who hurriedly explained that her fiancé was not stalking her mother. She elaborated that the checks on the bank and phone records had been done at her own behest, due to her mother's tendency to spend more money than she has. Additionally, she explained that her mother had a history of mental illness, and such incidents had occurred before. Officer Potts, after explaining that she still had to go inside to ensure Rachel's safety, was granted access to the house, which was revealed to be the house of Rachel's daughter and her fiancé. The Officer then took statements from the fiancé – who seemed thoroughly embarrassed by the whole incident – and Rachel, who maintained her contention of an inappropriate relationship but agreed not to press charges.

What piece of evidence presented to Officer Potts by Rachel did her daughter and her fiancé not provide an explanation for?
   a. Her claim that her daughter's fiancé was stalking her.
   b. Her claim that her daughter's fiancé was looking into her phone records.
   c. Her claim that her daughter's fiancé was looking into her bank records.
   d. Her claim that her daughter's fiancé was sending her explicit texts and pictures.

25. Officer Logan was the first officer on the scene of a drive-by shooting. Fortunately, no one on the street was hit, so after ensuring all civilians felt safe, he began to question eyewitnesses. According to one man, who was waiting by the intersection that the car drove by, there were three men in the car, two men in the front and one man in the back. He claimed that only the man in the back seat had a gun, and claimed he heard five shots in total. Another witness, who was on the other side of the street and further up the street, claimed there was a fourth individual in the back seat who was ducked down, and additionally claimed the passenger in the front seat had a gun as well. She couldn't remember exactly how many shots were taken, but claimed each man took at least one shot. She also pointed Officer Logan to the area where the car stopped to fire. Investigating the area, Officer Logan found eight shell casings in total. Additionally, there were two types of casing, five belonging to a smaller caliber and three belonging to a larger caliber.

Based on the evidence and eye witness testimony, how many shots did the passenger in the front seat mostly likely take?
   a. Five
   b. Eight
   c. Three
   d. One

121

Spatial Orientation

Use the following map for questions 1-5:

N

Ravine Park

Ravine Rd

W. Terrace Rd

Rose Ave

Cary Rd

Vista Hill Rd

Elliot Rd

Old Rd

Duxbury Rd

Station Rd

Forest Ave

Locust St

Bentley Rd

Old Colony Ln

Hutchinson Ct

Birch St

Station Rd

Beverly Dr

Croyden Ave

North Dr

Arleigh Dr

Nassau Dr

Plynouth Rd

Elizabeth M Baker Elementary School

East Dr

Warwick Rd

Devon Rd

Sutton Ct

Ruxton Rd

Allenwood Rd

West Dr

Fairview Ave

Cambridge Rd

Great Neck Village Office

Wooleys Ln

Oxford Blvd

Birdie Path

Colgate Rd

Memorial Park

Baker Hill Rd

Essex Rd

Croyden Ave

Piccadilly Rd

Radnor Rd

Shaar Zion of Great Neck

Bet Eliyahu Congregation of Great Neck

Memorial Field

Berkshire Rd

Patsy Pl

Wooleys Ln

Middle Neck Rd

Young Israel of Great Neck

Henry St

Great Neck Public School

St. Aloysius Roman Catholic Church

Nirvana Ave

Gould St

William St

Temple Beth-El of Great Neck

Polo Rd

122

1. You are driving in a car starting at the corner of Vista Hill Road and W. Terrace Road. Go north on W. Terrace Road. Take a right turn, then turn west. Take the second left. You are now closest to which of the following?
   a. Warwick Road and Allenwood Road
   b. Oxford Boulevard and Warwick Road
   c. Hutchinson Court
   d. Cary Road and Vista Hill Road

2. Which of the following is the shortest route from Great Neck Village Office to Ravine Park?
   a. Travel south on Cambridge Road, and turn right at the first intersection. Turn right onto Piccadilly Road, then proceed north to Fairview Avenue. Turn left, and proceed until you reach the park.
   b. Travel west on Baker Hill Road, then turn south onto Station Road. Take the second left onto Ravine Road, and proceed east until you reach the park.
   c. Travel south on Cambridge Road, and turn left at the first intersection. Take a right onto Plymouth Road, then take the first left. Follow Old Colony Lane onto Old Road, then turn south onto Station Road. Turn left, and proceed until you reach the park.
   d. Travel east on Baker Hill Road, then turn south onto Station Road. Proceed south until you reach Vista Hill Road, and turn left. Take the first left after W. Terrace Road, and proceed north until you reach the park.

3. Starting at the north end of Birdie Path, you take a left turn and walk along the road to the fifth intersection. There, you head east, and take a left turn at the first intersection. You take the first left turn. Where are you?
   a. Birch Street and Forest Avenue
   b. Forest Avenue and Station Road
   c. West Drive and Nassau Drive
   d. On a circular path

4. Which of the following gives the shortest directions from the intersection of Nirvana Avenue and Gould Street to the corner of East Drive and Arleigh Drive?
   a. Turn northeast onto Gould Street, then take the first right. Take a right turn onto Middle Neck Road, and proceed south past Shaar Zion of Great Neck. After Shaar Zion, take the third left turn, and head east onto Beverly Drive. Turn north onto East Drive, and stop after one block.
   b. Follow Nirvana Avenue southwest to Middle Neck Road, and turn right. Proceed south past the school, then take the third left turn. Head east onto Beverly Drive. Take a left turn on West Drive, then turn right onto Arleigh Drive. Keep going until you reach East Drive.
   c. Take Gould Street east, then turn right. Once you're on Middle Neck Road, turn left onto Piccadilly Road, and follow the road east until you reach Old Colony Lane. Keep going east until Station Road, then take a turn right. Follow Station Road as it curves west, then turn left. Take a quick right onto Arleigh Drive, and keep going until your destination.
   d. Take Gould Street east, then turn right onto Middle Neck Road. Take a left onto Wooleys Lane. Drive past Shaar Zion of Great Neck, then turn south onto Cambridge Road. Keep going south until you reach North Drive, and take a left. On North Drive, take the first right onto East Drive, and stop after one block.

123

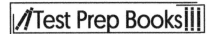

5. Starting from the intersection of Station Road and Baker Hill Road, drive west. Take the first turn north, then the first left. Proceed through three intersections, then take a left turn. At the next intersection, turn right. Take the second right, then proceed west. To which of the following landmarks are you closest?

    a.   Great Neck Village Office
    b.   Elizabeth M Baker Elementary School
    c.   Memorial Park
    d.   St. Aloysius Roman Catholic Church

Use the following map for questions 6-10:

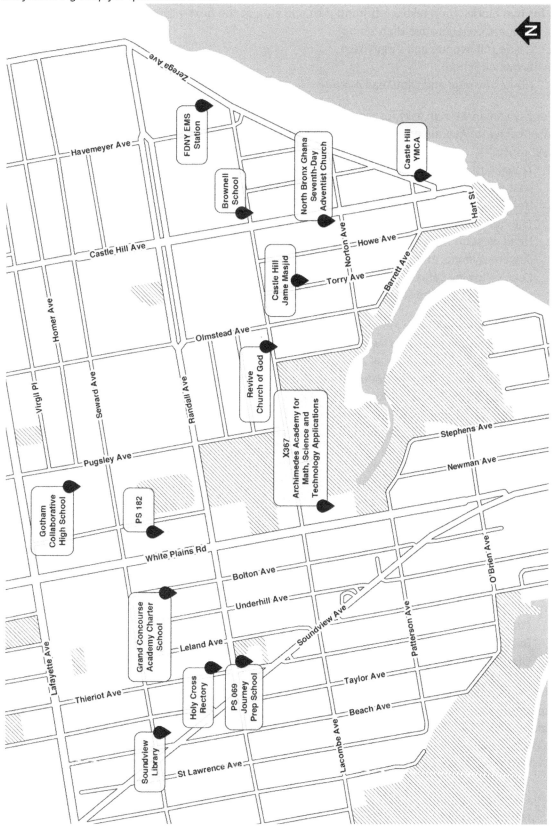

6. Starting from PS 182, you drive south. You turn east, then follow the road for three blocks. You turn north for two blocks, then take a left-hand turn and stop at the next intersection. Where are you?
   a. Gotham Collaborative High School
   b. Castle Hill Avenue and Virgil Place
   c. Brownell School
   d. Homer Avenue and Olmstead Avenue

7. A Pennsylvanian woman asks for directions to PS 069 Journey Prep School while standing at the corner of Lafayette Avenue and White Plains Road. Which of the following directions provides the simplest route?
   a. Travel east on Lafayette Avenue, then turn south at Thieriot Avenue. Follow Thieriot Avenue past Holy Cross Rectory. The school is on the left.
   b. Head south down White Plains Road to Seward Avenue, and turn right. Take a left turn on Thieriot Avenue, and proceed south until you reach the school.
   c. Head west on Lafayette Avenue, and take a left turn onto Thieriot Avenue. Turn left again on to Seward Avenue, and turn right down Bolton Avenue. The school will be on the right.
   d. Keep following Lafayette Avenue east, then take a right turn onto Pugsley Avenue. Once you pass Virgil Place, the school will be on your right.

8. What's the shortest route to get from the Castle Hill YMCA to the Soundview Library?
   a. Take Barrett Avenue northwest to Olmstead Avenue and proceed north on Olmstead Avenue. Take a left turn onto Randall Avenue, and turn right onto White Plains Road. Take a left on Seward Avenue, then proceed until you're at the library.
   b. Head north on Castle Hill Avenue, then turn left onto Seward Avenue. Keep going straight until you reach the library.
   c. Follow Castle Hill Avenue north to Randall Avenue, then head west through the intersection with White Plains Road. Turn northwest onto Soundview Avenue, and keep going until you see the library.
   d. Follow Castle Hill Avenue north past Randall Avenue. Take a left onto Virgil Place, then head north at the school. Take another left onto Lafayette Avenue. After the intersection with Thieriot Avenue, take the second left and go south until you see the library.

9. Walking south on Havemeyer Avenue from Homer Avenue, you take the second right turn, then turn left at the next intersection. You walk south, then turn west at the school. After three blocks, you stop. Which landmark is closest to your location?
   a. X367 Archimedes Academy for Math, Science and Technology Applications
   b. Castle Hill Jame Masjid
   c. Brownell School
   d. Olmstead Avenue and Lacombe Avenue

10. From Holy Cross Rectory, you head south past PS 069 Journey Prep School and through the first intersection. At the next intersection, you take a left turn and proceed until you've crossed the bridge. You take the first right turn, then follow the road eastward until it stops. What road did you take past North Bronx Ghana Seventh-Day Adventist Church?
   a. Castle Hill Avenue
   b. Zerega Avenue
   c. Lacombe Avenue
   d. Norton Avenue

Visualization

1. The suspect is believed to have grown a mustache since his last sighting. Which of the following is the same person?

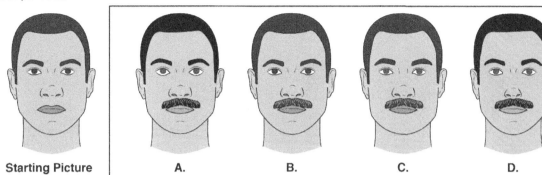

2. The suspect is believed to have lost weight recently. Which of the following is the same person?

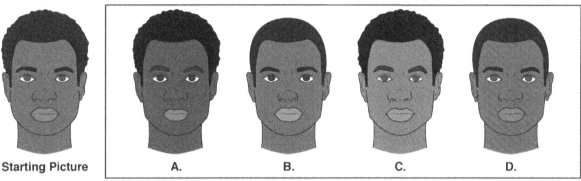

3. The suspect is reported to have started to wear glasses to make themselves less recognizable. Which of the following is the same person?

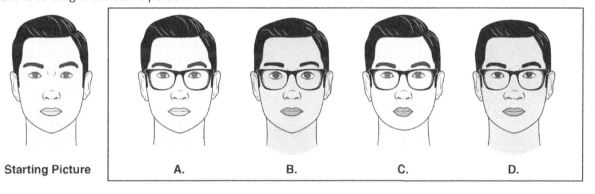

4. The suspect is reported to have significantly altered her hair in an unknown fashion. Which of the following is the same person?

Starting Picture   A.   B.   C.   D.

5. The suspect is believed to have forgone glasses for contacts. Which of the following is the same person?

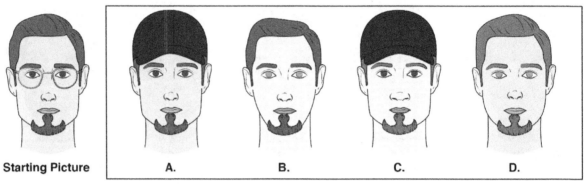

Starting Picture   A.   B.   C.   D.

6. The suspect is believed to have gained weight and added glasses. Which of the following is the same person?

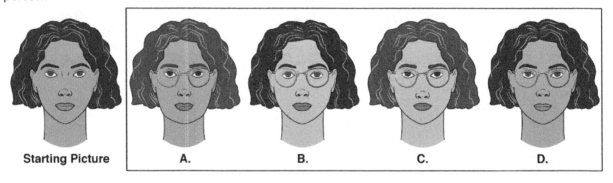

Starting Picture   A.   B.   C.   D.

7. The suspect is believed to have had a medical procedure to alter her lips. Which of the following is the same person?

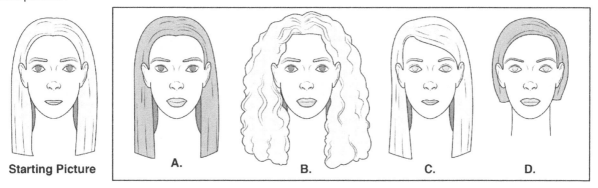

Starting Picture   A.   B.   C.   D.

8. The suspect is believed to have added a wig and glasses. Which of the following is the same person?

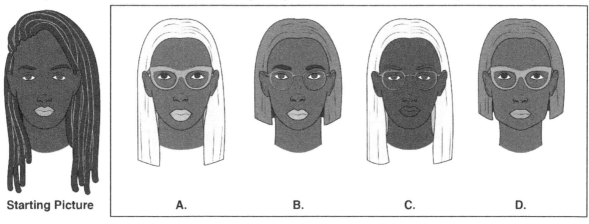

Starting Picture   A.   B.   C.   D.

9. The suspect is believed to have sustained an injury to their nose. Which of the following is the same person?

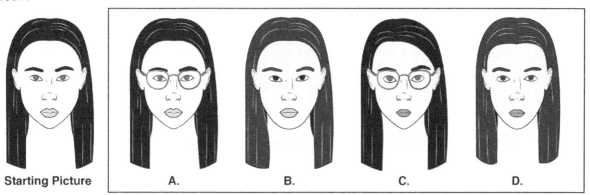

Starting Picture   A.   B.   C.   D.

10. The suspect is believed to have sustained scarring to his face. Which of the following is the same person?

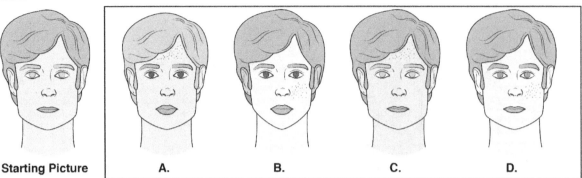

Starting Picture   A.   B.   C.   D.

Answer Explanations

Written Comprehension

1. D: Based on the passage, the most accurate statement is that some court records are sealed for reasons such as protecting the privacy of a minor involved in the case. While many court records can be accessed in online databases, some must be requested from a specific department such as the Appellate Court. The majority of court records are considered part of the public domain, but not all records are made public. Military status is part of court documents and can therefore be revealed through those records that are made part of the public domain.

2. A: Based on the passage, the most accurate statement is that each state makes its own laws about how and when court records can be accessed by the public. While a judge can seal a record for a minor, it is not required. Also, judges do have the power to seal a record, but this is usually only done in extraordinary circumstances. In California, only some court records are available through county databases. Appellate and Supreme Court records must be accessed through the Appellate Court.

3. D: Based on the passage, the new law discussed will add training in what to do at a traffic stop to driver's education courses in Illinois, so this is the best answer. The new law only adds this component to the courses; it does not require that all drivers take the course. The law does not target underage drivers, but aims to protect them from doing anything risky during a stop, so the goal is not to pull over more teens. While it is not advised that drivers reach under the seat or argue with the officer, it is not illegal. Drivers should know their rights and exercise them.

4. C: Based on the passage, the best answer is that traffic stop training is aimed to prevent drivers from panicking when they are pulled over. Traffic stops are actually one of the more dangerous parts of being a police officer. While a young driver may learn from a police officer during a traffic stop, the paragraph focuses more on how driver's education courses are being updated to instruct young drivers on how to handle a traffic stop. The paragraph is stressing a need for education in what to do during a traffic stop, so the last statement contradicts that point. A driver who believes he is driving safely could still be stopped.

5. D: This statement is the most accurate because the passage states that thirty-one states allow private citizens to open carry a firearm without a license. Thus, open carry laws are not very strict in all fifty states. California, Florida, and Illinois are singled out not because they allow open carry without a permit, but because they are the only states that prohibit open carry of a firearm. Because of these states' laws on open carry, the final statement about nineteen states requiring a permit cannot be true.

6. C: This is the most accurate statement because the passage asserts that all states including the District of Columbia allow for concealed carry of a firearm in public. The passage states that forty-two states, not eight, require a permit for concealed carry of a firearm in public. The "may issue" law allows states to pose more restrictions on who can be granted a concealed carry permit, while the "shall issue" law is much less restrictive.

7. B: The passage begins by stating the Miranda rights have been required since the 1966 Supreme Court case of Miranda v. Arizona, so this is the most accurate statement. The Miranda rights do not require the person in custody to remain silent, but notify them that they may remain silent if they choose to. Police officers must read the Miranda rights to any person in custody to protect the

131

information they may get in interrogation. The Miranda rights tell the person in custody that they have the right to an attorney and that one will be provided to them if they cannot afford an attorney.

8. C: This statement is the most accurate because the passage states that in order to comply with Miranda rights, a person in custody must waive their rights. Miranda rights protect both the person in custody and the police. They also protect the admissibility of the information gained in any questioning. While police officers could be sued for any number of reasons, the passage does not make any indication that they could be sued for not reading a person in custody their Miranda rights. When a person has not waived their Miranda rights, the information they provide may not be admissible in court.

9. B: The passage indicates that police departments can successfully use social media to identify suspects and find missing persons. The passage does not deter police departments from using any social media outlet. Trust can be built with the community when they feel they have a voice through police social media sites. The passage states that the use of social media by police departments is actually growing in popularity.

10. A: Based on the passage, this statement is the most accurate because it calls for a single point of contact to manage the sites for continuity. The passage actually calls for police departments to limit details on ongoing cases, but it does not say it is not beneficial in these cases. For example, the paragraph states that social media can be helpful in identifying a suspect, which would be for an ongoing case. That does not mean they should reveal all the details of the crime or anything that might jeopardize the case. While some departments may opt to hire a consultant to set up their social media sites, nothing in the paragraph suggests that this is necessary.

11. B: The correct answer is *B*. Cross-contamination has the potential to destroy any evidence collected and jeopardize any case a prosecutor may be hoping to build against a suspect. For that reason, it is one of the most important aspect of collecting evidence. Choice *A* is incorrect because failure to properly store evidence in an appropriate sealed container can result in damage to the evidence as well as, possibly, cross-contamination as well. Therefore, storage is equally important. Choice *C* is incorrect as while crime scene investigators play an important role, there is far more that goes into a successful prosecution that the collection of evidence. Choice *D* is incorrect as crime scene investigators are trained at determining what items at a crime scene are of evidentiary value. Collecting everything from a scene and then narrowing down what might be evidence would consume far too much time.

12. C: Choice *C* is correct. Monitoring the chain of custody is one of the essential elements of evidence collection as it ensures the integrity of the evidence. Choice *A* is incorrect as identifying a suspect comes after the crime scene investigation and once investigators have had a chance to gather and analyze the evidence. Choice *B* is incorrect. While avoiding cross-contamination is important, it is part of several steps (collection and storing) and not a step itself. Choice *D* is incorrect as it is not a step itself. Wearing gloves is important, but it is part of the collection process.

13. C: Choice *C* is correct. One of the goals of questioning a witness is to have them volunteer as much information as they possibly can and the best way to do that, without leading them, is to ask open ended questions. Choice *A* is incorrect. While open ended questions may create the opportunity to ask a follow-up, it's not the primary goal. Choice *B* is incorrect as open-ended questions may be effective on their own and not require a follow-up or close ended question. Choice *D* is incorrect as the goal is to not lead the witness to useful information. In fact, leading questions create reliability problems with the information provided and the information is not useful.

14. D: Choice D is correct. When preparing to interview witnesses at a crime or accident scene it is best to separate them to avoid them sharing their experiences. When they are not separated, they may talk about what they saw and that might change someone's story meaning you miss out on potentially important information. Choice A is incorrect. As noted, you don't want them sharing their stories as it may impact the stories they have to tell meaning you won't get a good picture of what happened. Different people will notice different things. Choice B is incorrect. While you do want to ask them open-ended questions, you want to separate them first. Overhearing another person's experience may taint someone's testimony. Choice C is incorrect. You want to make sure you gather evidence while it is fresh in their memory. This passage does not discuss letting them leave prior to gathering evidence.

15. B: Choice B is correct. The passage identifies both organization and clarity as the two most important elements of report writing. Choice A is incorrect. While details are important in the report, how they are organized is paramount. Choice C is incorrect. While concise is a great quality in good writing, it shouldn't come at the expense of other elements of the report, such as organization, clarity, and even including all the details and information. Choice D is incorrect. While organization is important, it may not be best to use the victim's timeline rather than a linear order of events as they happened. For example, a witness may have seen something prior to the victim which may change the organization and timeline.

16. D: Choice D is correct. Determining the timeline to use and the best way to present the events as they happened is a huge challenge. Multiple people may present multiple timelines and efforts to tell them all at once will impact clarity. Choice A is incorrect. The evidence can be reported at the end and is, therefore, not a challenge. Choice B is incorrect. While notetaking and remembering witness's recollections is important, it's not presented as a challenge here. Choice C is incorrect. While including relevant information and facts in the report is crucial, it's not noted as the biggest challenge in the passage. In fact, the passage notes that the end of the report presents an opportunity to include information which may be relevant.

17. A: Choice A is correct. According to the passage, the best time to include evidence that may not be included in witness reports is at the end of the report. Choice B is incorrect as evidence may be lost within the story and impact both organization and clarity. Choice C is incorrect as at the start, it may not be clear how information is related to the events or why something is evidentiary. Therefore, evidence should be included at the end, when its connection to the crime is, hopefully, clearer. Choice D is incorrect. While other reports regarding evidence may be required, evidence relevant to the crime should be included in the original report. The passage does not discuss additional reports.

18. A: Choice A is correct. The passage notes three reasons why someone might be nervous to testify and lack of control is one of those reasons. Choice B is incorrect. In fact, the passage notes that familiarizing oneself with the information and facts alleviates anxiety. Choice C is incorrect. While public speaking is easier with more experience, it's not noted in the passage nor is it clear that this is referencing experience public speaking vs. testifying. Choice D is incorrect. While that might have an impact on one's anxiety, it's not noted in the passage.

19. D: Choice D is correct. The passage notes a few ways to alleviate the anxiety and fear of testifying and reviewing the facts and laws is one great way. Choice A is incorrect. There is no mention of that in the passage, though there is mention that an attorney may research an officer. Choice B is incorrect. While that might be useful in familiarizing an officer with the experience, it's not noted in the passage. Choice C is incorrect. While practicing public speaking is a good tact, and might be inferred from the information given in the passage, it is not listed in the passage specifically as a step.

20. B: Choice *B* is correct. The last thing an officer should want is for a prosecutor to be caught off guard or to not be prepared for questions related to their personnel file. For that reason, officers should be open with those involved in the case, such as prosecutors, regarding any marks or reports that may be found in their personnel files. Choice *A* is incorrect. The prosecutor should have the facts of the case based on police and investigator reports. Choice *C* is incorrect. What an officer might have learned about an attorney or judge isn't particularly relevant, and it is likely other attorneys have access to the same information. Further, the passage doesn't discuss that solution. Choice *D* is incorrect. While revealing one's anxiety might be helpful and allow a prosecutor to help an officer prepare, it's not discussed in the passage.

Written Expression

1. C

2. C

3. B

4. D

5. D

6. B

7. D

8. B

9. C

10. D

11. A

12. D

13. B: *Stealing* and *embezzling* are synonyms.

Stealing: the act of taking a thing from somebody that isn't one's own

Embezzling: to defraud someone or to steal property (often money) entrusted into one's care

14. A: *Cleared* and *exonerated* are synonyms.

Cleared: to be absolved of misunderstanding or doubt

Exonerated: to be pronounced not guilty of criminal charges

15. C: *Death* and *fatality* are synonyms.

Death: the event of a person's life ending

Fatality: a death that occurs as the result of an accident, disaster, war, or disease

134

16. D: *Fake* and *forgery* are synonyms.

Fake: an imitation of reality; a simulation

Forgery: to create or imitate something (e.g., an object or document) with the intent to deceive others or profit from the sale of it

17. A: *Hidden* and *latent* are synonyms.

Hidden: something kept out of sight or concealed

Latent: a thing that's hidden, or something that exists but hasn't been developed yet

18. B: *Postponement*: to hold off on a scheduled activity until a later date

Moratorium: a legal postponement or waiting period set by some authority to suspend activity

19. C: *Criminal*: someone who is guilty of a crime

Perpetrator: the person who commits a crime

20. C: *Lie*: to state a contradiction of the truth; to deceive

Prevaricate: to deliberately evade the truth or lie in order to mislead

Memorization

1. B

2. C

3. D

4. B

5. A

6. B

7. C

8. D

9. C

10. B

11. B

12. D

13. A

14. D

15. C

16. D

17. B

18. C

19. A

20. B

Inductive Reasoning

1. B: Choice *B* is correct because multiple provisions in paragraph (e) are used to seek objective metrics that indicate the relationship's emotional strength (such as the duration of the relationship). Choice *A* is incorrect because family members need not have minors in their household. Choice *C* is incorrect because paragraph (e) specifies that persons in an intimate relationship need not have lived together. Choice *D* is incorrect because consanguinity is not a determining factor in paragraph (e).

2. D: Choice *D* is the most reasonable answer because the definition covers a variety of close relationships with diverse types of family bond. This breadth makes the definition useful for a crime that may take place in a variety of household structures, such as domestic violence. Thus, Choice *D* is correct. Choice *A* is incorrect because sections of the passage are not concerned with minors. Choice *B* is incorrect because the passage defines more relationships than needed by the tax code to determine if an individual is single or married. Choice *C* is incorrect because the passage does not define the space within which a family or household might live.

3. C: Choice *C* is correct because the phrase "assistance or intervention" encapsulates all the results of interaction provided in the "contact" definition. Choice *A* is incorrect because the definition indicates that the Patrol Guide does describe how officers should have conversations with individuals. Choice *B* is incorrect because it does not take into account situations in which an officer must intervene due to the behavior of the person experiencing homelessness. Choice *D* is incorrect because the definition does not require the officer to have initiated the interaction.

4. A: Choice *A* is correct because the passage references reckless behavior by minors (i.e., drinking) as a possible exigent cause for warrantless entry. Choice *B* is incorrect because the passage does not indicate that minor violators are more or less dangerous than adults. Choice *C* is incorrect because the provision about devices owned by minors indicates that complaints about noise violations by minors are not rare. Choice *D* is incorrect because the answer is not an inference about minors.

5. C: The officer is required to provide the violator with a copy of their summons and the receipt for their seized property. Choice *C* is correct because the summons includes the number of violators but does *not* list the violators' ages. Choices *A, B,* and *D* are incorrect because the officer is required to provide all three pieces of information to the violator.

6. B: Choice *B* is correct because the answer adequately generalizes the exigent dangers summarized in section (VII). Choice *A* is incorrect because the officer may only seize the device if they have lawful access—in other words, a warrant. Choice *C* is incorrect because allegations of sexual assault are listed

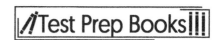

as an exigent condition. Choice *D* is incorrect because noncompliance is not listed as grounds for warrantless entry.

7. B: Choice *B* is correct because a reasonable explanation for notifying Missing Persons at this stage in the procedure is to ensure good communication about the child's whereabouts. This ensures the child will be reunited with their guardians as soon as possible. Choices *A* and *C* are incorrect because the process to return the child should logically begin when the child is first brought to police. Choice *D* is incorrect because if the child's location is known, they cannot logically be "missing."

8. A: Choice *A* is correct because the guidance applies to both prisoners and victims. Consequently, the requirement of confidentiality is not altered by an individual's criminal status. Choice *B* is incorrect because the guidance does not indicate that prisoners are subject to different rules. Choices *C* and *D* are incorrect because the purpose of confidentiality cannot be logically inferred from this passage.

9. A: The question specifically asks for when vehicle break-ins occur; therefore, to determine the correct choice, the data that relates specifically to vehicle break-ins should be examined. From the given information, most vehicle break-ins happen at the strip mall along Lakeshore School Road on Wednesdays from 5:00 p.m. to 9:00 p.m., so the best time to prevent these break-ins would be to arrive at the location an hour early and stay an hour later to catch all potential break-ins.

10. C: This question is regarding only house break-ins, which, according to the data given, occur between Roosevelt and Van Buren on Mondays from 10:00 a.m. to 2:00 p.m. The remaining choices, although the time or day may be correct, do not list the correct area according to the report.

Deductive Reasoning

1. B: Choice *B* is correct because both individuals are related by blood, and because they are both minors, it is probable that they live in the same household. Choice *A* is incorrect because the relationship is not consanguineous. It is worth remembering that consanguinity is not the only criterion for a family offense—however, this criterion is what this question seeks. Choices *C* and *D* are incorrect because the consanguineous individuals do not live in the same household.

2. A: Choice *A* is correct because the crime fails the 3-Part test on the basis of causing significant injury. Choice *B* is incorrect because the accused is under the age of sixteen. Choice *C* is incorrect because this is not a violent crime, and their motion was filed after thirty days had passed. Choice *D* is incorrect because the crime is a misdemeanor.

3. D: Choice *D* is correct because the use of threats qualifies as violence, but the crime does not involve physical injury, a weapon, or sex offenses. Choice *A* is incorrect because the crime caused significant injury. Choice *B* is incorrect because the crime was not violent, and the 3-Part test is only applied to violent crimes. Choice *C* is incorrect because the crime was a sex offense.

4. C: This case will most likely begin in the Youth Part, and then be transferred to the Family Court after thirty days. The Family Court does not try or sentence persons under eighteen as adults. Thus, Choice *C* is correct. Choices *A* and *B* are incorrect because the case will likely be transferred to the Family Court. Choice *D* is incorrect because the Family Court will not sentence the accused as an adult.

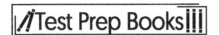

5. D: Choice *D* is correct because the suspect is short and of legal age to be in a nightclub, which serves alcohol. Choice *A* is incorrect because the suspect is too tall. Choice *B* is incorrect because the suspect is not 21 or older. Choice *C* is incorrect because the suspect is an employee, not a stranger.

6. B: Choice *B* is correct because when the suspect seized the officer's firearm, access to that weapon constituted an imminent danger to the officer and other persons around them. Choice *A* is incorrect because the strike is not considered deadly force. Choice *C* is correct because using the firearm unreasonably puts bystanders at risk. Choice *D* is incorrect because it is reasonable to assume the officer can neutralize the threat without use of deadly force.

7. C: Choice *C* is correct because the suspect's hands on the officer's chest reasonably appeared to the officer like an imminent threat to his life via asphyxiation. Choice *A* is incorrect because noncompliance does not warrant deadly force. Choice *B* is incorrect because the suspect was no longer driving. Choice *D* is incorrect because the account does not provide details about the physical characteristics of the officer and the suspect.

8. A: The crime that could possibly relate the most to this case, based on the driver's slurred speech and irresponsible driving, would be that she is intoxicated. It is described that her papers are in order, implying her insurance was up to date, making Choice *B* incorrect. Choice *C* is incorrect because even though the state law had regulated the speed limit in the area to 45 mph, the driver could not be considered to be speeding if she was only driving 5 mph over the limit. Choice *D* is also incorrect because there is no indication the driver is suicidal.

9. D: Although not explicitly stated in the scenario, the logical outcome will most likely result in the underage drinking of minors as defined by the statute. The remaining choices, although possible crimes in their own respect, still do not match the statute given because they cannot be related to the incident in a logical way.

10. A: Even though the mother's state of mind may be questionable, it does not relate to the case of the missing child and will do little to help solve the problem. Choice *B,* the information about the lost bike and money may lead to where the child may have gone, and Choice *C,* the time of night, and Choice *D,* the name of the mother, are important details to frame the background of the story.

11. C: Discovering what type of paraphernalia was possibly used could lead to a cause of death and is the only information relevant to the man's death. The remaining choices, although detailing information related to the scene, have no direct influence on the case of how the man died and do not provide insight on how the case can be solved.

12. A: Gang violence could involve multiple, dangerous individuals, so for the officer's protection it would be best to call for backup in this instance. Choice *B*, Choice *C*, and Choice *D* all are minor, non-violent crimes involving few people; therefore, they would not necessarily require an officer to call for backup assistance.

13. D: Only if the officer has very reasonable cause to further investigate an individual should they take such action. However, if the smell of alcohol is too strong for an officer not to miss, there is a just cause in asking the individual to step out of their car because they could possibly be intoxicated and cause harm to others while behind the wheel. Choice *A*, Choice *B*, and Choice *C* do not give enough evidence that the driver is suspicious of anything other than a minor traffic violation.

14. A: The fact that repeats itself most often in each of the witness's reports is that the shooting took place around the workers' lunchtime, which was noon. There is also little reason indicated as to why the witnesses would lie about the time. The remaining choices, although they may also be true, are not verified by the repeated accounts of the different witnesses.

15. B: The only witness who does not contradict some of their information or is not too emotionally involved in their details is witness 2 because they are able to give a clear, concise detailing of what they observed on the day of the crime. Their answers are given in an honest way that does not try to actively deny any events that took place in a defensive way.

Information Ordering and Problem Sensitivity

1. B: Choice *B* is correct because logically, the officer will contact dispatch before taking any of the other listed actions. Choice *A* is incorrect because the officer is unlikely to perform the actions needed to speak with a mechanic (such as calling or traveling there) prior to contacting dispatch. Choice *C* is incorrect because the officer turned the key twice successfully, so they are unlikely to have the wrong key. Choice *D* is incorrect because the officer is unlikely to call a tow service prior to contacting dispatch.

2. C: First, organize the information and events from the passage in chronological order:

First, Mr. Robert May exited the subway car and stopped, attempting to orient himself. He first turned right, looking at a set of stairs he quickly identified as leading to a different subway transfer than the one he needed to take. Then, Mr. May turned to his left, and saw that the stairs to the subway transfer he needed were to his left.

Next, Mr. May was bumped into by a man walking directly at him. The individual had been walking from Mr. May's left side to his right, so that the collided front on when Mr. May turned to face the left staircase. Both men dropped several items they were holding, at which point Mr. May bent down and set his computer bag aside.

At some point among the confusion, another individual, who had been walking alongside the man who bumped into Mr. May, reportedly picked up Mr. May's bag. The individual continued to walk in the direction the men had been heading before the collision occurred. The individual head up the staircase that was originally to Mr. May's right, which led to the transfer Mr. May did not intend to use.

Recognizing that his bag had been taken, Mr. May attempted to pursue the individual who he believed had taken it, following them up the staircase. However, Mr. May struggled to keep up with the individual, and upon leaving the station, found no sight of the individual. Mr. May then returned to the station and reported what had occurred to Officer Wilcox.

Choice *C* is correct because Mr. May claimed he saw the individual heading in the same direction as the man Mr. May bumped into was headed. Choice *A* is incorrect because there was no mention that the individual went onto the train. Choice *B* is incorrect because Mr. May claimed to have followed the man out, so it would make no sense for the individual to have remained on the track. Choice *D* is incorrect because Mr. May claimed the individual did not turn back around but kept walking forward.

3. B: First, organize the information and events from the passage in chronological order:

First, three individuals who appeared to be drinking companions entered the liquor store. They pooled their money to buy some liquor, which the group then took outside the liquor store to enjoy.

139

Next, a verbal altercation broke out, according to the cashier inside the liquor store. Apparently, the individuals began to bicker and debate how much each individual was drinking. The physical altercation broke out soon after that, with the cashier reporting hearing expletives and the sound of glass shattering. The store owner then quickly called 911 and Officer Mullen was dispatched to the scene.

Officer Mullen first conducted an interview with the cashier, who explained to the Officer what she had witnessed, as well as what she knew about the individuals as frequent customers.

Next, Officer Mullen went out and attempted to interview the three individuals involved in the incident. Two of the individuals, a man and a woman, refused to speak with the officer, but the third individual, who appeared to be the victim of the attack, did agree to speak. They informed the officer that the other individuals were "bad friends", that they had previously tried to steal money from them, and that the attack itself occurred when the woman present had hit the individual over the head with the half full bottle of liquor they had been bickering over. As the individual spoke with Officer Mullen, the Officer assessed the individual's injuries, which included a gash about their right eye and a number of smaller, more superficial wound.

After taking the first individual's statement, Officer Mullen then took statements from the other two individuals, the man and the woman, who seemingly wanted to defend themselves from the accusation. The man present claimed the attack was in reality an accident, and specifically that the bottle had slipped. Before the man could finish his statement, the woman interrupted, informing Officer Mullen that the other individual present was lying about what had happened, and in fact that they were the ones attempting to steal from the other two present.

Choice B is correct because the individual claimed the other two individuals were "bad friends" who were always trying to take their money, and that the woman had brought a half full bottle of liquor down on top of their head. Choice A is incorrect because that is what the man who the Officer spoke with after the first individual claimed. Choice C and Choice D are both incorrect because no mention was made by any individual involved in the incident that the altercation was caused by anyone feeling jealous of anyone's relationship.

4. D: Choice *D* is correct because the principal is expected to submit a complete report to the police. Choices *A, B*, and *C* are incorrect because the listed tasks are the duty of the sergeant.

5. A: Choice *A* is correct because per section (VIIC) the sergeant ought to submit a report to the principal that the records do list the incident and indicate that it was not a qualifying incident. Choice *B* is incorrect because the report has been found. Choices *C* and *D* are incorrect because the sergeant is not required to investigate if the alleged crime was or was not a qualifying incident.

6. D: Choice *D* is correct because the only time the passage directs the sergeant to contact a detective is if the report is unclear about whether the allegations were unfounded. Choices *A, B,* and *C* are incorrect because none of those steps require the sergeant to receive clarification from a detective.

7. B: Choice *B* is correct because section (IIFii) indicates that the process for recording an individual finger begins with centering the finger on the small platen. Choice *A* is incorrect because the finger is rolled after centering it. Choice *C* is incorrect because the four fingers are printed collectively prior to the individual prints. Choice *D* is incorrect because the check digit is entered prior to beginning the fingerprinting process.

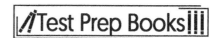

8. D: Choice *D* is correct because section (IIAi) directs the officer to moisten the prisoner's hands with a Pre-Scan Pad if necessary. Choices *A* and *B* are incorrect because the process for cleaning the LIVESCAN machine is not provided in this passage. Choice *C* is incorrect because the process for ensuring the prisoner's hands are clean is not specified—the Pre-Scan Pad is only specified in case of excessive dryness.

9. C: First organize the information and events from the passage in chronological order:

First, at some point before Ms. Townsend arrived home to her apartment, her estranged friend gained access to her apartment. Ms. Townsend testified to Officer Gonzales that she believed her friend most likely gained access to the apartment through a window in the bathroom, which she claimed was typically left open and easily accessible from the back of the building. The estranged friend seemingly went about tossing many of Ms. Townsend's items into large trash bags and depositing it them into the hallway outside the apartment. Additionally, Ms. Townsend put the chain latch on the door at some point before Ms. Townsend returned home.

Next. Ms. Townsend returns home from a party, sometime early in the morning on Wednesday, January 6th. As she approaches her apartment door, she notices several large trash bags in the hallway outside her door. She then approached the bags and inspected them closer, and found them to be full of many of her personal possessions. Ms. Townsend then attempted to gain access to the apartment, but found that the chain latch was on. Ms. Townsend called out, to which she testified she heard her friend respond, but the friend did not come to the door.

After realizing the severity of the situation, Ms. Townsend then proceeded to call 911, and at 3:34AM, Officer Gonzales arrived. She explained the situation with her friend and the current situation in the apartment. Officer Gonzales then approached the apartment and, using a key provide by Ms. Townsend, attempted to gain entry. He similarly found the door was chain latched, and also could hear loud music playing. He then loudly identified himself, to which he then heard the music stop and the estranged friend coming to the door. Finally, the estranged friend apologized to the Officer, and Ms. Townsend declined to press charges.

Choice C is correct because the bathroom window was usually open. Choice A is incorrect because Ms. Townsend did not claim to have given the friend a key. Choice B is incorrect because Ms. Townsend could not have chain-latched her door from outside. Choice D is incorrect because there was no mention of a broken window, and it would be unnecessary if the window was typically open.

10. C: First, organize the information and events from the passage in chronological order:

First, the concerned citizen called 911, and told the operator he wanted to report a case of suspected parental abuse. He then explained that this had been an ongoing situation, and that he often heard both parents yelling at their two children. The caller estimated the children to be approximately 9 and 12 years old. The caller then reported that on other occasions he had heard the children yell out and a loud male voice quick tell them to be quiet, and the caller believed that the children were screaming out in pain. Furthermore, the caller attested that he believed the mother and grandmother living in the apartment also physically disciplined the kids. He also identified another individual living in the apartment, an older male figure he had seen on multiple occasions. Finally, the caller explained that he was prompted to call when he encountered one of the children on their way to school, and he saw they had a black eye.

141

Choice C is correct because the caller claimed to have witnessed two children, a mother, father, grandmother and another older male figure residing in the apartment. Choices A, B, and D are all incorrect because they neglect to include one or multiple of the individuals the caller claimed to have witnessed – mostly likely either one of the parents and/or the grandmother and additional older male figure present.

11. A: First, organize the information and events from the passage in chronological order:

First, at a quarter past four in the afternoon, a group of individuals wearing identical ski masks entered the bodega and proceeded to grab as many items as they could and quickly leave. As the individuals were in the midst of grabbing up the items, a number of other people in the bodega, including the cashier and an officer at a local fire station, attempted to stop them. The officer, specifically, attempted to grab the items out of an individual's hand, at which point several other of the individuals involved in the robbery grouped up and pushed the officer against a freezer. The individuals then fled, and someone called 911 to report the incident.

Soon after, Officer Jefferson arrived at the bodega to investigate. The Officer spoke to the cashier present at the time of the robbery, who identified himself as Tito. Tito both told the Officer what he had witnessed as well as presented the Officer with the security camera footage that corroborated what Tito had told him. Additionally, Tito told the Officer that he believed the robbers to be students at a local high school, that he had seen them before, and that he could easily identify the individuals if needed.

Choice A is correct because Tito claimed that he seen the individuals before, and he believed them to be local high school students. Choice B is incorrect because the fire station officer mentioned was attempting to stop the robbery, not commit it. Choices C and D are both incorrect because Tito did claim to know who the individuals were, and Choice C is additionally incorrect because he did claim he could identify them if needed.

12. D: First, organize the information and events from the passage in chronological order:

First, a number of reports were made to 911 dispatchers regarding suspicious activity at an empty lot. One common theory that dispatchers noted was that the area was being used by drug dealers and their customers.

As a result, Officers Lewis and Powell were dispatched to the lot, and arrived at around 1:30pm. The Officers found no individuals present at the site, but did find evidence of illicit drug use, specifically hypodermic needles and marijuana joint filters. They reported on what they saw and continue their normal patrol.

That night, several more calls were made to 911 regarding activity in the lot, and one caller specifically told the dispatcher they had seem armed individuals at the site.

At 2:30am, Officers Martin and Machado were sent to check out the site again. The Officers found a group of individuals on the empty lot who appeared to be attempting to hide. The Officers then established contact with the individuals, and discovered them to a be group of drug users. The individuals claimed, and the Officers found no evidence to the contrary, that there was no selling of drugs occurring on the site, only the usage of drugs. The Officers then informed the individuals that the lot was privately owned, meaning they were technically trespassing, and that a significant number of reports had been made about their activities already. With that knowledge, the individuals agreed to leave the lot.

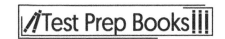

Choice D is correct because the first officers to inspect the empty lot, Officers Lewis and Powell, found only evidence of illicit drug use at the site. Choice A is incorrect because no officers encountered armed individuals at the empty lot, and that claim was only made by one report made to the police. Choice B is incorrect because that is what the second set of officers, Officers Martin and Machado, discovered upon arriving at the scene. Choice C is incorrect because no officers found any evidence of drug dealing in the empty lot, and the only claims made to that effect were from reports made to the police.

13. B: First, organize the information and events from the passage in chronological order:

Officer Beasley responded to a report of a physical altercation in a park between two intoxicated individuals.

Upon arriving at the scene, Officer Beasley began by speaking briefly to the two men involved in the altercation, who identified themselves as Oliver Foley and Alec Gardner, before interviewing an independent bystander and eyewitness. She attested to the Officer that she had watched the two individuals having a verbal altercation for several minutes, with Mr. Foley standing off to the side of a path and Mr. Gardner seated on a park bench. The eyewitness then informed Officer Beasley that she had witnessed Mr. Gardner stand up off the bench and walk towards Mr. Foley, who then pushed Mr. Gardner back against the bench.

Officer Beasley then spoke with Mr. Foley first, who claimed that the fight began when asked Mr. Gardner if he could sit next to him on a public park bench. Mr. Foley claimed that Mr. Gardner then became increasingly upset with Mr. Foley, and began to insinuate that Mr. Foley was a prostitute. Mr. Foley claimed the physical fight began when Mr. Gardner stood up off the bench and bumped into him, causing Mr. Foley to react by pushing Mr. Gardner back.

Officer Beasley then finished by speaking with Mr. Gardner. Mr. Gardner claimed to the Officer that Mr. Foley had approached Mr. Gardner attempting to solicit sex from him. Mr. Gardner furthermore claimed that he had then immediately refused and stood up off the bench, to which Mr. Foley attacked him, pushing him back down.

Choice B is correct because the independent bystander claimed she had witnessed the fight begin after a few minutes of verbal interaction between the two men. Choice A is incorrect because no one at the scene claimed the men had been in a verbal altercation for more than a few minutes when the fight broke out. Choice C is incorrect because that claim was made by Mr. Gardner. Choice D is incorrect because no one at the scene claimed the men did not speak to each other because their physical altercation began.

14. D: First, organize the information and events from the passage in chronological order:

Officer Orozco was dispatched to a construction site that had reported possibly stolen equipment and spoke to the foreman of the site, a Mr. Kelly Phillips. Mr. Phillips then reported to Officer Orozco the following series of events.

First, prior to any actual planning or construction on the site, there was community outrage regarding the site, since it had once been a local institution that had failed to pay its rent and closed, and additionally that the community was not pleased with the new plans for the site either.

143

When inspection first began on the site, Mr. Phillips reported to Officer Orozco, there was a widespread vandalization of the surveying equipment, and several of the pieces had gone missing and presumably been stolen.

When construction began on the site, there was a brief period where there was verbal harassment of the construction workers themselves, though Mr. Phillips claimed this wasn't a prolonged or particularly prevalent phenomenon either.

Over the next few weeks of the project, Mr. Phillips then reported seeing more and more items going missing from the site, from extra tarps to protective materials to building material. Initially, Mr. Phillips had not reported the items as missing to the police, as the company responsible for the project was willing to simply replace the items.

However, Mr. Phillips had reported recently finding several large construction tools, including jackhammers, missing from the site, at which point he made the decision to call the police.

Choice D is correct because Mr. Phillips claimed the first items to go missing from the construction site were pieces of surveying equipment that had been either stolen or vandalized before the actual construction had begun. Choice A is incorrect because no valuables were stolen from construction workers, and the resentment aimed at workers never went beyond harassment. Answer B is incorrect because those items had gone missing over after construction had started, after the theft of the surveying tools. Answer C is incorrect because the theft of those items is what finally prompted Mr. Phillips to call the police, well after many other items had already been stolen from the site.

15. A: First, organize the information and events from the passage in chronological order:

Officer Anderson was dispatched to an apartment due to the resident reporting having been witness to a home invasion. Upon arriving at the scene, the Officer spoke with the caller, who identified herself as Edith Terrell. Ms. Terrell then identified the apartment, which was the ground floor apartment across the street from Ms. Terrell's apartment. She explained to the Officer that although she did not directly know the individuals living in the apartment, she had seen them on occasion, and believed them to be a family with school aged children. Additionally, she testified that she had not seen the anyone in the family at home in a number of days. She then recounted what he had seen to Officer Anderson.

Shortly after arriving home to her own apartment, Ms. Terrell happened to notice that the front door to the apartment across the street had been propped open, and that all the lights were all on. Knowing what she knew about the family living in that apartment, Ms. Terrell at first assumed that perhaps the family was in the middle of returning home from vacation.

Sometime after that, however, Ms. Terrell reported seeing four men wearing full face respirators flee the apartment with what appeared to be full duffel bags.

Choice A is correct because the first irregularity Ms. Terrell claimed she noticed was that the door to the apartment was propped open and all the lights in the apartment were on. Choice B is incorrect because Ms. Terrell had not communicated with the family regarding their vacation, and therefore would not know when they were supposed to return. Choice C is incorrect because no members of the family were even seen by Ms. Terrell during the home invasion. Choice D is incorrect because Ms. Terrell only saw the men leave the apartment well after she was alerted to something going on in the apartment.

16. C: First, organize the information and events from the passage in chronological order:

First, the disgruntled customer arrived at the coffee shop. Multiple individuals familiar with the customer claimed she had a personal vendetta against one of the baristas working there, and that she had come to the coffee shop attempting to confront her. The customer did then attempt to confront the barista, who told the customer they did not want to speak with them further.

Next, the manager of the coffee shop becomes involved, asking the customer to leave the coffee shop, as her actions were making the barista and others uncomfortable. In response, the customer reportedly sat on the floor and refused to move. The manager allowed the customer to remain sitting on the floor for a period of time, although eventually asked the customer to leave once more when she began harassing other customers and telling them to not tip their barista.

It was at this point that the manager made the decision to call the police, and subsequently the customer was informed. Once the customer was informed that the police were on their way, she reportedly became aggressive, which ended with her physically restraining the barista and pouring hot coffee on her.

Shortly after, Officer Fisher arrived at the coffee shop, where she found a screaming match ensuing between the manager and the customer. Officer Fisher then proceeded to escort the disgruntled customer, before taking statements from the customer, the manager, the barista, and a number of witnesses.

Choice C is correct because the manager claimed that when the customer was first asked to leave the coffee shop, they sat on the floor and refused to leave. Choice A is incorrect because although the customer told other customers not to tip the barista, she did not physically touch the tip jar itself. Choice B is incorrect because the customer only assaulted the barista once she was informed the police were on their way. Choice D is incorrect because the customer had refused to leave until Officer Fisher arrived and escorted her out.

17. C: First, organize the information and events from the passage in chronological order:

First, a number of pilots and other employees at a small regional airport reported being flashed by lasers on the runway, and a 911 call was made by one of the employees. In the call, the individual claimed that they had witnessed teenagers sneaking in through a hole in the fence that ran along the runway near a heavily wooded area. Additionally, the caller claimed the airport had had similar problems in the past.

Officer Delacruz was then dispatched to the airport, and began by inspecting the site at which the caller had claimed to have seen the teenagers. Although no one was there, they did find evidence of recent activity, including cigarette butts, beer cans and marks in the ground identified as being left from the stakes of a camping chair.

The next day, more reports of lasers being flashed were made, and Officer Delacruz was again dispatched as a result. Returning to the same spot, they this time noticed two camouflaged individuals in the wooded area. Officer Delacruz then announced themselves and the individuals came out. The two men claimed they were hunters who had stumbled across the area the day prior, and furthermore claimed to have been heavily drinking.

Choice C is correct because the 911 caller claimed to have seen teenagers sneaking in through a hole in the fence. Choices A and D are incorrect because no employee of the airport was ever accused by anyone of being responsible for the laser flashings. Choice B is incorrect because the hunters were only

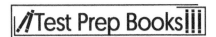

revealed as being responsible once Officer Delacruz had investigated the area on two separate occasions.

18. D: First, organize the information and events from the passage in chronological order:

Prior to the estranged parent entering the child care center with a knife, there were eight children present with four adults overseeing them.

When the man first entered, he met with the director in the front officer. Also present were his son and another child, who was in the front office in order to use the first aid kit. He demanded the child be released to him, to which the director refused. The man then barred the front door.

Although barring the front door prevented those in the office from easily escaping, there was a back entrance which could be accessed through the main room, where the rest of the children and adults were. They quickly became alerted to the presence of the man and fled through the back door. It was at this point, presumably, that the 911 call was first made.

At some point after this, Officer Gutierrez arrived at the scene and was briefed on the situation by another officer present.

Choice D is correct because by the time Officer Gutierrez arrived on the scene, the only individuals that remained in the building were the estranged father and the three remaining hostages, which consisted of the director of the center, the man's child, and another child who was in the front office using the first aid kit. Choice A is incorrect because although that was the initial number of individuals when the estranged father first barred the door, six children and three adults were quickly able to leave through a rear exit. Choices B and C are both incorrect because they neglect to include some of the hostages still inside, either the other child or the director and the child.

19. A: First, organize the information and events from the passage in chronological order:

An eyewitness testified seeing the man passed out on the train for several stops before becoming aggressive when jostled awake by the train.

Eyewitnesses then attest that the man had begun acting aggressive towards others, and in particular that he had been waving a glass bottle of what appeared to be liquor at other passengers. Eyewitnesses additionally reported that most of the other passengers had left the car in response to the man's aggressive actions.

Soon after, Officers Cohen and Johnson arrived on the scene, locating the man in the final few cars of the train. They noticed that there was a broken glass bottle of liquor on the floor, and when they attempted to speak with the man, they found him to be mostly incoherent. From what they could gather, it seemed that the man had believed someone had intentionally woken him up, and that from there everything else was just a misunderstanding.

Choice A is correct because the other passengers on the train claimed the man had been sleeping prior to being aggressive, and that he had only become aggressive once awoken by the jostling of the train itself. Choice B is incorrect because the man himself had been sleeping, and therefore could not have been waking up others. Choice C is incorrect because the man had become aggressive immediately upon waking, and had been seemingly drinking since boarding the train. Choice D is incorrect because the man had been seen asleep on the train by several eyewitnesses.

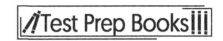

20. B: First, organize the information and events from the passage in chronological order:

First, a concerned citizen called 911, refused to identify herself but claiming she had seen armed gang members in and around a school she lived nearby. When asked to clarify what she had seen exactly, the caller explained that she had witnessed a group of young men smoking a joint on the blacktop outside of the school. When then asked specifically to identify the number of men and the number of weapons, the caller said she could not recall and that she in fact had not actually seen the guns, but could tell the men were armed from the way they stood.

As a result of this call, Officer Cunningham was dispatched to the high school. Upon not seeing any immediate signs of active gang activity, Officer Cunningham then proceeded to speak to a school administrator about the claim.

The school administrator told the Officer that the school did have a problem with certain students skipping class to smoke, but that she was fairly certain no students were carrying weapons, as the school was equipped with metal detectors.

Next, Officer Cunningham examined the site the 911 caller had identified, and found a number of half-smoked joints. He also encountered a custodial worker taking a smoke break, who claimed he was familiar with the students who skipped school to smoke, and that he knew they were not armed or gang affiliated.

Choice B is correct because the 911 caller claimed to police that she had witnessed armed gang members in and around the school's property. Choice A is incorrect because she made no mention of marijuana smoke initially, and when asked to clarify she claimed that she directly witnessed individuals smoking a joint. Choice C is incorrect because she claimed the individuals were gang members, not custodial workers. Choice D is incorrect because while she did claim the men were armed, she did not claim to have seen them wielding or aiming their weapons directly.

21. D: First, organize the information and events from the passage in chronological order:

Two individuals, a middle-aged man and woman, arrived at a public park with a vibrant orange blanket and proceeded to both ingest hallucinogenic drugs.

At some point after that the two individuals got in a disagreement, at which point the woman stormed off, according to the man.

Sometime soon after that, the woman was seen by eyewitnesses in the park stripping off her clothes and attempting to go swimming in a park fountain. She remained in that state for at least half an hour, eventually resorting to running about a large open green area naked while several onlookers stopped and gawked, with a few even attempting to help the woman out.

It was at this point that Officers Love and Hansen first arrived at the scene, and attempted to approach the woman and calm her down. When their presence seemed to only agitate her further, the Officers backed off and proceeded to speak to the eyewitnesses, one of whom told the officers they had seen the woman a few hours prior in a different area of the park. They furthermore claimed they could identify the blanket the woman had brought with her, and with that led the officers to the area she had mentioned.

Once there, the eyewitness identified the blanket they had seen the woman on, and the Officers saw that there was a man sleeping on the blanket. Upon questioning him, the Officers learned that the two had come to the park together to take hallucinogenic drugs, and that he hadn't seen the woman since she had stormed off after an argument they had.

Choice D is correct because the eyewitnesses in the park claimed the woman had initially stripped because she intended to go swimming in the public fountain. Choice A is incorrect because eyewitnesses reported watching her strip down. Choice B is incorrect because no eyewitnesses were aware of her boyfriend or the fight they had been having. Choice C is incorrect because no eyewitnesses had seen her take hallucinogenic drugs, and therefore they did not know.

22. A: First, organize the information and events from the passage in chronological order:

First, Officers Yang and Hawkins received notice while on patrol near a subway station that a group of young men had been shaking down passengers and those on the subway platform. They proceeded to the station, where they flagged down a station employee.

Upon speaking to the station employee, they were informed that the men had positioned themselves down to one side of the station, and that they were positioned near an exit. The employee additionally claimed that he believed if the group saw the officers, they would all be able to quickly get away via the exit nearest to them.

With this knowledge, Officer Yang positioned himself near the exit the individuals would come through if they ran in the direction the station employee claimed they would. Once he was in position, Officer Hawkins entered the station and approached the group of men, who were where the station employee had claimed they were.

Upon approaching the men, they quickly identified him and began to flee. Although Officer Hawkins wasn't exactly sure how many individuals there were due to how quickly some of them fled, he saw at least some of them leaving in the direction of Officer Yang.

Officer Hawkins then saw that multiple individuals were running right at him. He was able to detain two of the individuals who ran at him, but counted another three who evaded capture. Officer Hawkins then detained and handcuffed both individuals he had captured.

Upon regrouping with Officer Yang, Officer Hawkins was informed that an additional four individuals had left through the exit he had been manning, and that he had been able to detain of them.

Choice A is correct because Officer Hawkins saw five individuals and detained two, while Officer Yang saw four individuals and detained three. Choice B has an additional man unreported by either Officer. Choices C and D claim no one evaded capture, but both Officers had individuals evaded capture.

23. B: First, organize the information and events from the passage in chronological order:

First, a young woman made a call to the police, reporting that she suspected her neighbor of being a serial killer. She then provided the following information to the operator.

First, she informed the officer that she was new to the neighborhood, and that a number of home invasions and assaults of woman in the area had her feeling more on edge and vigilant.

She then explained to the operator what she had witnessed the previous night. Upon returning home to her apartment building after a night shift, the young woman had been greeted in the lobby by the young man who lived across the way from her. She said she was a bit shocked to have met anyone in the lobby at so late an hour, but became further concerned when she noticed he had blood on his shirt sleeves, which were visible under his parka.

Later that night, the caller claimed she heard the sound of a woman screaming and heavy machinery coming from the man's apartment. She furthermore informed the officer that she had rarely seen the man except at night, believing him to be pretty reclusive.

Following the 911 call, Officer Hudson was dispatched to the man's apartment, and spoke to Mr. Igor Belyaev. Mr. Belyaev told Officer Hudson that he had recently immigrated from Europe, and had been working night shifts at his uncle's butchers' shop. He claimed the blood stains on his shirt were from work, and he preferred to just toss a parka over it until he was home.

When asked about his activities the following night, Mr Belyaev claimed he had had trouble sleeping that night after work, and had endeavored to work on a personal carpentry project in order to tire himself out.

Choice B is correct because Mr. Belyaev made no mention of the anyone screaming in his apartment, or why someone would have heard that. Choices A and C are incorrect because he explained them both by explaining to the officer that he was working night shifts at his uncle's butchers' shop. Choice D is incorrect because he explained that he was up late working on a carpentry project while unable to sleep.

24. D: First, organize the information and events from the passage in chronological order:

First, the mother of a young woman, identifying herself solely as Rachel, entered the police station, filing a report with Officer Potts.

In the report, the woman claimed her daughter's fiancé was stalking her. She first explained that she had long suspected her daughter's fiancé of wanting to sleep with her. Rachel then provided evidence to Officer Potts, including evidence that her daughter's fiancé had been monitoring her bank and phone records, and explicit texts and pictures that appeared to be from the fiancé. Officer Potts then informed Rachel that she would be looking into it, and that she would feel safe returning home knowing the police were looking into it.

Rachel then made another call to Officer Potts shortly after, in which she claimed the fiancé was waiting for her when she returned home. Officer Potts then made her way to the address Rachel had provided the Officer.

Upon arriving to the address, Officer Potts was greeted by a woman who introduced herself as Rachel's daughter, and who then attempted to explain to the Officer that her fiancé was not stalking her mom.

According to Rachel's daughter, the checks of the bank and phone records had not been conducted by her fiancé, but by herself. She then explained to the Officer that her mother had a history of mental illness, and similar incidents had occurred previously.

149

After taking the daughter's statement, Officer Potts was granted access to the house, which she found out belonged to the daughter and her fiancé. Officer Potts then spoke with the embarrassed fiancé and Rachel, who maintained her accusations but agreed to not continue with the accusation of stalking.

Choice D is correct because neither Rachel's daughter or her fiancé mentioned an explanation for the explicit texts and pictures provided to Officer Potts. Choice A is incorrect because Rachel's daughter explained that her mother had a history of mental illness and doing similar things in the past. Choices B and C are incorrect because Rachel's daughter explained to Officer Potts that she was the one checking her mother's bank and phone records.

25. C: First, organize the information and events from the passage in chronological order:

First, the drive-by shooting occurred. Officer Logan then arrived on the scene and ensured there were no serious causalities. Luckily, no one was hurt and two eyewitnesses later gave their accounts to Officer Logan as to what they saw.

According to one eyewitness, a man who had been waiting at the intersection the car drove by, there were three men in the car – two men sitting in the front and another man in the back. The eyewitness told Officer Logan he had only seen the man in the back seat wielding a gun, and that he had heard five shots go off.

According to the other eyewitness Officer Logan spoke to, a woman located on the opposite side of the street from the previous eyewitness, there was a fourth individual in the car as well, who had been ducking down in the back next to the other man in the back. Additionally, the woman claimed that the man in the front passenger's seat had also had a gun, and claimed each man shot at least once, although she wasn't certain how many shots were taken in total. She also pointed out to the Officer where the car had stopped to shoot.

Examining this area, Officer Logan found eight shell casings, five belonging to one caliber and three belonging to a large one.

Choice C is correct because one witness claimed he saw the individual in the back seat shoot five times, and there were five casings belonging to one type of caliber and three casings belonging to the other caliber. Choice A is incorrect because that is the number of shots likely taken by the man in the back seat. Choice B is incorrect because that is the number of total casings recovered. Choice D is incorrect because each caliber type was fired more than once.

Spatial Orientation

1. B: This route starts out going north on W. Terrace Road, but then the road turns west without an intersection. Because each of the southbound streets would be a left turn, you don't turn right until W. Terrace Road reaches Station Road. After turning right on Station Road, the west turn takes you down Wooleys Lane. The first left is on Plymouth Road, while the second is on Warwick Road. The directions lead you most closely to the intersection of Oxford Boulevard and Warwick Road because they turn left off of Wooleys Lane onto Warwick Road, approaching Oxford Boulevard. Therefore, Choice *B* is correct. Since no mention was made of going any farther, we can't logically assume that the directions ended at Allenwood Road. Thus, Choice *A* is incorrect. You could also reach the incorrect Choice *A* by turning left at the intersection of Station Road and W. Terrace Road. Choice *C* makes the mistake of taking the second left off Station Road and is incorrect. Choice *D* makes the mistake of reading W. Terrace Road as

150

ending when it stops going north, rather than continuing to Station Road. Without additional labels, W. Terrace Road is logically the road that carries straight through those intersections, rather than Elliot Road, Cary Road, or Rose Avenue.

2. C: Choice *C* is correct because this set of directions is the shortest route to Ravine Park that is also accurate. Choice *A* is incorrect because the directions lead to Memorial Park. Choice *B* is incorrect because you need to travel east on Baker Hill Road, not west. Choice *D* is incorrect because the route is longer than the directions given in Choice *C*.

3. D: Choice *D* is correct because these directions lead onto an unlabeled circular path to the left of Birch Street. Choice *A* is incorrect because the walker stopped at the right turn off of Birch Street instead of proceeding to make the final left turn. Choice *B* is incorrect because the walker proceeded too far along Station Road. Choice *C* is incorrect because the walker proceeded south along West Drive, rather than east along North Drive.

4. A: Choice *A* is correct because this set of directions is the shortest route to East Drive and Arleigh Drive that is also accurate. Choice *B* is incorrect because Nirvana Avenue goes southeast, not southwest. Choice *C* is incorrect because these directions are not the shortest route. Choice *D* is incorrect because Cambridge Road does not have an intersection with North Drive.

5. B: Choice *B* is correct because these directions lead the driver to head west along Croyden Avenue toward Elizabeth M Baker Elementary School. Choices *A*, *C*, and *D* are incorrect because each landmark is farther from the destination than the school.

6. D: The directions lead to the corner of Homer Avenue and Olmstead Avenue. Thus, Choice *D* is correct. Choice *A* is incorrect because the directions do not reach Gotham Collaborative High School. Choice *B* is incorrect because the directions turn west on Homer Avenue. Choice *C* is incorrect because the directions lead north on Castle Hill Avenue, not south.

7. B: Choice *B* is correct because this set of directions provides the simplest instructions while also being accurate. Choice *A* is incorrect because the woman ought to go west on Lafayette Avenue, not east. Choices *C* and *D* are incorrect because both sets of directions lead to an incorrect school.

8. A: Choice *A* is correct because it describes a northwest route that most directly leads from the Castle Hill YMCA to the Soundview Library. Choices *B*, *C*, and *D* are incorrect because they each head farther north than needed to create the shortest route.

9. B: The directions lead to the intersection of Olmstead Avenue and Lacombe Avenue. As the Revive Church of God is not listed among the answer options, the next-closest landmark is Castle Hill Jame Masjid. Thus, Choice *B* is correct. Choice *A* is incorrect because the directions do not lead that far west along Lacombe Avenue. Choice *C* is incorrect because the directions walk past Brownell School but end closer to another landmark. Choice *D* is incorrect because the answer indicates an intersection, not a landmark.

10. D: Choice *D* is correct because the right-hand turn after the bridge was made at Revive Church of God, and following the road leads onto Norton Avenue past North Bronx Ghana Seventh-Day Adventist Church. Choice *A* is incorrect because the route does not follow Castle Hill Avenue. Choice *B* is incorrect because Norton Avenue is used to pass the church, arriving at Zerega Avenue at the end of the route. Choice *C* is incorrect because the route crosses the bridge while on Lacombe Avenue and only later passes by the church.

Visualization

1. B: The correct answer is Choice *B*, as this is the same face but with a mustache. Choice *A* is incorrect, as this person has differently shaped eyes. Choice *C* is incorrect, as this person's jawline is different. Choice *D* is incorrect, as this person's nose shape is different.

2. D: The correct answer is Choice *D*, as this is the same face but with less full cheeks as if the individual had lost weight. Even with the shaved head, his facial characteristics remain consistent with the starting picture. Choice *A* is incorrect, as, despite having the same hair style and less full cheeks, this person has closer-set eyes. Choice *B* is incorrect, as this person has a narrower nose. Choice *C* is incorrect, as this person has narrower eyes.

3. A: The correct answer is Choice *A*, as this is the same face but with glasses. Choice *B* is incorrect, as this person has a different eye shape. Choice *C* is incorrect, as this person has a different face shape. Choice *D* is incorrect, as this person has a different nose shape.

4. C: The correct answer is Choice *C*, as this is the same face but with a different hairstyle. Choice *A* is incorrect, as this person has a different jawline. Choice *B* is incorrect, as this person has a different nose. Choice *D* is incorrect, as this person has a different eye shape.

5. A: The correct answer is Choice *A*, as this is the same face without glasses and with a baseball cap. Choice *B* is incorrect, as this person has a different jawline. Choice *C* is incorrect, as this person has a wider nose. Choice *D* is incorrect, as this person has a different face shape and a shorter nose.

6. D: The correct answer is Choice *D*, as this is the same face but with large, wire-rimmed glasses and fuller cheeks as though the person has gained weight. Choice *A* is incorrect, as this person has a different jawline. Choice *B* is incorrect, as this person has a different eye shape. Choice *C* is incorrect, as this person has a different nose.

7. B: The correct answer is Choice *B*, as this is the same face but with fuller lips, which the person could have obtained with the medical procedure. Choice *A* is incorrect, as this person has a different eye shape. Choice *C* is incorrect, as this person has a different nose. Choice *D* is incorrect, as this person has a different chin shape.

8. C: The correct answer is Choice *C*, as this is the same face but with a wig and glasses on. Choice *A* is incorrect, as this person has a different nose. Choice *B* is incorrect, as this person has a different eye shape. Choice *D* is incorrect, as this person has a different jawline.

9. A: The correct answer is Choice *A*, as this is the same face but with a different nose, which likely resulted from the person's injury. Choice *B* is incorrect, as this person has a different chin shape. Choice *C* is incorrect, as this person has a different eye shape. Choice *D* is incorrect, as this person has a different face shape and eye shape.

10. C: The correct answer is Choice *C*, as this face is the same aside from the scarring. Choice *A* is incorrect, as this person has different lips. Choice *B* is incorrect, as this person has a different jawline. Choice *D* is incorrect, as this person has a different eye shape.

Dear NYPD Test Taker,

Thank you again for purchasing this study guide for your NYPD exam. We hope that we exceeded your expectations.

Our goal in creating this study guide was to cover all of the topics that you will see on the test. We also strove to make our practice questions as similar as possible to what you will encounter on test day. With that being said, if you found something that you feel was not up to your standards, please send us an email and let us know.

We would also like to let you know about another book in our catalog that may interest you.

Civil Service

This can be found on Amazon: amazon.com/dp/1637758561

We have study guides in a wide variety of fields. If the one you are looking for isn't listed above, then try searching for it on Amazon or send us an email.

Thanks Again and Happy Testing!
Product Development Team
info@studyguideteam.com

FREE Test Taking Tips Video/DVD Offer

To better serve you, we created videos covering test taking tips that we want to give you for FREE. **These videos cover world-class tips that will help you succeed on your test.**

We just ask that you send us feedback about this product. Please let us know what you thought about it—whether good, bad, or indifferent.

To get your **FREE videos**, you can use the QR code below or email freevideos@studyguideteam.com with "Free Videos" in the subject line and the following information in the body of the email:

      a. The title of your product

      b. Your product rating on a scale of 1-5, with 5 being the highest

      c. Your feedback about the product

If you have any questions or concerns, please don't hesitate to contact us at info@studyguideteam.com.

Thank you!

Made in United States
North Haven, CT
12 March 2025

66707585R00089